Violence as Good
For Those Who Commit It

A Reader

Jane F. Gilgun, Ph.D.

Also by Jane Gilgun

Books

The Logic of Murderous Rampages & Other Essays on Violence & its Prevention
Chicago School Traditions: Deductive Qualitative Analysis & Grounded Theory
Child Sexual Abuse: From Harsh Realities to Hope
Children with Serious Conduct Issues
I Want to Show You: Poems
On Being a Sh*t: Unkind Deeds & Cover-Ups in Everyday Life
The NEATS: A Child & Family Assessment

Children's Books

Busjacked!
Emma and her Forever Person
Five Little Cygnets Cross the Bundoran Road
Salamander: A Story of Two Boys
The King's Toast
The Little Pig Who Didn't go to Market
Will the Soccer Star

Short Pieces

An Intellectual History of Grounded Theory
Attachment & Child Development
Coding in Deductive Qualitative Research
Detecting the Potential for Violence
Neurobiology, Trauma, & Child Development
Reflexivity & Qualitative Research
Talking to Children Who Have Been Sexually Abused
The Sex Education of Children
Two Boys, Similar Backgrounds: One Goes to Prison & One Does Not: Why?
What Sexual Abuse Means to Child Survivors
What Sexual Abuse Means to Abusers
What Child Sexual Abuse Means to Girl & Women Perpetrators

Manuals

Lemons or Lemonade: An Anger Workbook for Kids
Lemons or Lemonade: An Anger Workbook for Teens
Readiness to Adopt Children with Specials Needs
CASPARS: Tools for Assessing Client Strengths & Risks

Contents

Introduction

A few months ago, after more than 30 years of interviewing persons who have committed violent acts, I realized that perpetrators think they are doing something good when they sexually abuse children, beat and rape their wives, get into bar fights, or commit murder.

The people I interviewed were decent men almost all of the time. They were fathers and husbands who took good care of their families, held responsible jobs such as bank executive, teachers, social workers, health care providers, truck drivers, and store managers. They enjoyed the love and respect of families and friends. They believed they loved their spouses, intimate partners, and children. Much of the time, they didn't see the harm.

A common explanation for violence is that persons who commit it had experienced violence themselves as children. They are hurt and distressed.

Childhood abuse and neglect as an explanation falls short. Many people are treated badly in childhood, and they do not harm others. They had experiences that helped them to cope with, adapt to, and overcome risks. They became resilient. They had people in their lives they trusted and they could talk to. Talking to others helped. The people in their lives were prosocial. They admired these people and wanted to be like them.

They also had protective factors that stopped them from acting on thoughts of violence that most if not all people have from time to time. In short, most people who experience the trauma of child abuse and neglect do not become violent.

Persons who commit violent acts do so because they think their actions will result in something good for themselves and, sometimes, for others. No one helped them to think and act otherwise. Many people think about doing violence. Those who do not carry out their thoughts consider consequences, Thoughts of consequences stop them from doing what they are thinking. They don't want to harm themselves and others.

For some people, the idea of violence as good may not be new. Lots of people might know this. After all, who doesn't take satisfaction in vengeance or in righting a wrong? Every day billions do, not only in movies and video games but in real lives.

People who commit violence either don't think about or don't care that others are hurt and their lives may end or be ruined. What they care about is what they want at the moment.

I hope these readings help others think about violence in new ways. It is clear that punishment and prison do not deter violence. It's time for new thinking.

I am a professor, School of Social Work, University of Minnesota, Twin Cities, USA. I have been doing research on the development of violent behaviors, the meanings of violence to perpetrators, and how persons overcome adversities for more than 30 years.

Jane F. Gilgun
9 January 2015
Minneapolis, Minnesota, USA

1

Violence as Good for Those Who Commit It

The world's religions are based on love and compassion. Those who commit violence almost always see themselves as devout practitioners of their religions. How do they turn compassion and love into hatred and vengeance? The interview research I have done for more than 30 shows that people who commit violence believe they are doing something good. Is this what we want?

Violence is a good thing for those who commit it. The persons who abducted three Israeli teenagers on June 12 of this year congratulated themselves and sang after they shot and killed the boys. The cellphone that one of the boys had used to call police to say they had been abducted was still on and transmitted to Israeli police the sounds of the rifle shots and the joyous aftermath.

The persons who abducted an Arab teen early in July, set him on fire, and left his burned body in a Jerusalem forest also thought they were doing a good thing—revenge for the killing of the three boys.

The smiling teen girls who held a sign that said, "Hating Arabs is not racism. It's values" showed the pleasure they took in hatred and the tacit approval they gave to the burning death of the Arab teen.

These are recent examples of violence as a good thing. Human beings throughout the world celebrate violence every day. Pro-violence forces are strong indeed.

The other sides of violence are the experiences of survivors. The parents, families, and friends of the murdered Arab and Israeli boys are in mourning. Arabs and Jews together say we have to stop killing and hating each other. Yet, enough people, Jews and Arabs, believe that violence is a good thing that the revenge killings will go on. Some want to kill teenagers. Some support bombings and rocket strikes on civilian populations. Some encourage children to throw stones on armed soldiers.

Violence as a solution becomes part of the problem. Violence from one side of a conflict provokes revenge in those who are the targets. When the response of the targets is violence, good comes to them but to few others. Such actions, supported by beliefs and the satisfactions of revenge, become a self-propelled cycle that has no end and no good consequences except a temporary sense of satisfaction and a twisted kind of comfort in doing to others what has been done to them.

Men who molest children, rape women, beat their wives and partners, who get into bar fights, are aggressive on highways, who cheat and life in business transactions—they are part of this cycle of violence. Women are part of the cycle, too, usually through words and not through sexual and physical attacks. They can be quick to perceive injustice when there is none. They can go on the attack and inflict emotional damage and desires for revenge in their targets.

How mindless this all is. Violence begets violence. Hatred begets hatred. Many if not most of the people who commit acts of violence not only believe they are doing something good but they also think they are religious. Major religions are based on compassion and love. Many say that God dwells within, or a holy spirit dwells within, or we are made in the image and likeness of God. The spirit of goodness is in us all, say major religions. We experience the spiritual dimension of human life when we love one another and see one another as children of the spirit.

How can someone who is a member of such religions look at another human being and then commit an act of violence? It seems as if a switch goes off. No longer are other people children of God, filled with the spirit, worthy of love. They are objects of hatred. They are worthy of vengeance, targets of rage. They are the other. They are not children of God.

It is easy to justify vengeance, outrage, and disgust at others. It is easy to be self-righteous. It is easy to be cruel to others when we define them as unworthy of respect and deserving of hatred.

All of the major religions encourage prayer and meditation. Through prayer and meditation we get in touch with peace, love, and harmony. We are supposed to bring these peaceful, loving states into our everyday interactions with others. Something helps us to turn off the switch of love and peace and lets us put ourselves into hatred and vengeance.

Is this what we want? Is this what the founders of our religions want? Is this what we want to leave to the world after we are dead?

Reference

Kershner, Isabel (2014). Arab boy's death escalates clash over abductions. *New York Times*, July 2. Downloaded July 3. http://www.nytimes.com/2014/07/03/world/middleeast/israel.html?action=click&contentCollection=U.S.&region=Footer&module=Top News&pgtype=article

2

What Violence Means to Perpetrators:
A Radio Interview

When perpetrators commit violence, they think they are doing something good. Sounds strange, I know, but read this interview, and you will see what I mean.

Hello, everyone and welcome to our show. I'm your host. It's my pleasure to introduce you to my next guest. A professor at the University of Minnesota School of Social Work. Everyone, Professor Jane Gilgun. Professor Gilgun, thank you for joining me.

Jane: Thank you.

Interviewer: A pleasure to have you on our show today. I will be speaking about circumstances affecting many cities throughout our nation, and that is the high rate of violent crimes, murders and abuse to children. For many folks who are listening in today, many of those folks who have been involved and experienced this who are—of course have noticed and seen it through their news outlets. Give us some insight through your research and understanding on this circumstance, and why it's happening on such a high level.

Jane: Well, my research area is on what violence means to perpetrators. And so I think if we can understand what it means to perpetrators we can figure out how to respond. What's really hard to believe about violence is when people commit violence they think they're doing something good. For example, when perpetrators of child sexual abuse sexually abuse children, many of them really think this is love. They can go on and on about how much this is love, you know, while the kids are thinking what's going on. You know, I'm uncomfortable, I don't like this.

It can be very scary to the children. That's contrary to what we believe about violence. Even in murder, when people commit murder, even when

10

they commit murder of people that they love, at the moment they're doing it, they really think that this is a good thing, and they really feel good about it. Then a few minutes later they realize what they did. But it's too late. So they have to live with what they've done. And when kids, you know, young people in gangs, when they're beating each other up and having fights and murdering, they do get a great deal of satisfaction out of it. [Minimalist?] much of the time. Some kids really don't want to participate, but they feel pressured into it, and it they don't participate they won't be part of the gang, and they'll be out on their own, and they want to be part of the gang. So not all gang violence, for the people who are part of it, find it a good thing, but they feel forced into it.

But some people who are in gangs really do think beating other people up and shooting them is a really good thing. Some of them, after they do it, feel terrible, but again, it's too late. So we really have to figure out how to help people realize that no matter what a good idea it might seem at the time, you really need to look two days down the road and see how you're going to feel then, and how what you're thinking of doing is going to affect other people. So it's a very difficult problem. There's no easy answer to this. When people are convinced they're doing something good, it can be very hard to have them think about other ways of getting what you want. Who doesn't want to feel good. Everybody wants to feel good, but do you have to feel good by hurting somebody else. That's the question.

Interviewer: You're so right about that. With that being the case, with this information, how do we take it and use it to be able to prevent these circumstances I'm sure for many of our listeners, that's really what we want to see be done.

J: Well, prevention, you know, there are a lot of people, and probably many listeners, who are doing prevention. You know, prevention is extremely difficult, because there are so many forces that lead to violence. I mean, we're a very—in a way, we like violence as a culture. We like to go to violent movies. We like to see car crashes. We like to see the good guys blow the bad guys to smithereens. Even on an everyday life, if somebody does something to us, we want to get back at them. So violence using guns and knives and fists is just that same sort of mentality, just bigger. On a bigger scale. If I'm mean to somebody because they were mean to me, well that's one thing. That's not very nice, but it's not like killing them or sexually abusing them. Or beating them up. But it's still the same type of thing. So, you know, one thing that everybody can do is start reflecting on themselves. Do they seek vengeance? Do they bear grudges?

11

Do they model that for their children? That's a really basic thing that everybody can do. And I do think, you know, rallies and marches and lobbying and organizing, is a really good thing, but at the same time we have to say ok, we don't like this, we don't like that, we don't like the fact that this eight year old kid sitting on the couch watching TV got shot in the head. We don't like that. But what are we going to do about that? And so it takes a lot of thought. And we've been thinking about it for a long time. But I do think it does begin with the individual.

But then we have to say well, what can people do. What kind of programs can we develop to help people think about keeping your self-respect in another way. There are many ways that we keep our self-respect. And violence is just one of them. There are many others, like just calling somebody out and saying, you know, you're acting like a—you're acting like you are entitled to something, and you know, you're just like everybody else. You're a worthy human being. You don't have to run around proving it. You already are. There are all kinds of things that we need to figure out that we haven't, to respond to this strong, strong mentality we have in this country about, oh, you know, you got to respect me. You can't disrespect me. If you do, there are going to be consequences. It's like, come on, aren't there other ways of making sure people respect you? You can start by respecting yourself. That's a really good start. But then of course we have to create a society where people feel respected, and that's a big issue.

Interviewer: Yeah.

Jane: That's huge.

Interviewer: Particularly when it comes to young people. I've heard, in my own circle many a time that that is the root cause of, you know, behind the acting out, the violent, and the conflict, is a lack of respect.

Jane: Right. It's a lack of respect, but then, it's also what they think they're supposed to do to get respect.

Interviewer: Mhm.

Jane: So, we have to start with helping kids feel respected automatically. When somebody disrespects them, they immediately think, what's the matter with you? I'm already worthy of respect. Why are you acting as if I'm not?

Interviewer: I see.

Jane: But, if kids don't have that response—what's the matter with you when you disrespect me—that's the kind of thing we have to figure out how to teach. To realize when somebody's disrespectful has nothing to do with you. It means they're just being jerks.

Interviewer: Correct. And your response is all that really matters in that circumstance. Of course you disrespect yourself when you act out in a way that is uncivilized.

Jane: But that's not how they see it, and that's what's really important. When you act out in ways that hurt others, you are doing what you're supposed to do, according to group norms, according to what people really think.

Interviewer: Yeah.

Jane: You can't get away with treating me this way, and I'm going to show you. That's a matter of self-respect too for a lot of people. And we think, we have to figure out how to help people assert their right to respect without hurting others.

Interviewer: Well, that—

Jane: That's the issue.

Interviewer: Well said.

Jane: Yes, absolutely everybody has the right to respect. Everybody must be respected. But the issue is, how do we help people feel that they're already respected and accepted and then how do we help them tell the other people, you're really acting ridiculous. Everybody's worthy of respect, even you, even when you act like a jerk.

Interviewer: Professor, I have to say, it does seem to some extent that [in] today's society and the age we live in, you [are] fighting an uphill battle in the efforts that you're speaking of. But we still want to continue that fight nonetheless. For folks who are listening in, particularly for those who are involved in education or impacting the lives of these young people—social workers, counselors, those who are involved in mental health and the like, we definitely want to encourage them to learn a lot more about the work that you're doing, the research you have, and to be able to assist you in your efforts. To do so, how can they get in contact with you?

Jane: I'm at the University of Minnesota, and I'm very easy to find on the internet. All you have to do is put my name in the internet. All kinds of stuff comes up. I've got a lot of free stuff, really free stuff.

Interviewer: Excellent. We definitely want to encourage folks to get in contact with you. I want to thank you again, Professor, for coming on the program today and speaking with us with this important message.

3

Two Brothers: One a Mass Murderer and the Other a Certified Public Accountant: What Makes the Difference?

A 20 year-old man murdered 20 first graders and six adults at Sandy Hook Elementary School in Newtown, Connecticut, USA, on December 14, 2012. Then he shot himself dead. Earlier that day he had shot and killed his mother with whom he lived. His older brother, a certified public accountant, is devastated. How can two young men with the same parents and raised in the same family and hometown turn out so differently?

Protective Factors

What makes the difference between persons who develop violent behaviors and persons who do not when they have similar backgrounds? In a few words, the difference is the existence of protective factors. Many people have risks for violence, but those who don't commit violent acts have protective factors that immediately spring into action. Protective factors are processes that help us to cope with, adapt to, and overcome risks.

This is how protective factors work. Many people have spontaneous outbursts when angry, such as "I could kill you" and spontaneous thoughts about hitting, kicking, and punching others. Just as spontaneously dire consequences for others and the self come to mind. They stop. Some even laugh at themselves for being so ridiculous. Thoughts of consequences stop them in their tracks. These are protective factors.

Some people think their thoughts of violence are great ideas. Thoughts of dire consequences for others and the self do not come to mind. Rather thoughts of the delights and satisfaction of violence to themselves spring up, spurring them into action. Violent people enjoy thinking about hurting others and believe they have good reasons for doing so. They often experience satisfaction and gratification, even chills and thrills.

People who don't stop themselves consider short-term consequences for themselves. If they think about longer-term consequences for themselves and consequences for others, they immediately dismiss them. The consequences that matter to them are their own gratification, satisfaction, thrills, chills, and a sense of accomplishment. If they think about the harm they cause, they may feel even more thrilled or they may not care. Some tell themselves the consequences are worth the price of the thrill and satisfaction of violence. They have tunnel vision. They only consider one part of a large picture. They do not think about how their violence will affect those they target or themselves in the long run.

Glee as a Risk

Survivors of mass murders are shocked to see the gleeful manner of the murderers. Crystal Woodman, a student at the Littleton, Colorado, USA, High School, where student gunmen killed 12 students and a teacher, reported about the gunmen: "every time they'd shoot someone, they'd holler, like it was, like, exciting." Nick Foss, another student, reported, "They were laughing after they shot. It was like they were having the time of their lives."

Fourteen year-old Barry Loukatis, killed a boy who had teased him. He also killed two other boys. He said, "It sure beats algebra, doesn't it?" as he stood over a dying boy who was choking on his own blood. According to an accomplice to five of his murders, Genildo Ferreira de Franca, a Brazilian who killed 15 people, laughed after each murder. Not only are protective factors missing at the time of the violent acts, but the thrill of the kill is an alluring and satisfying risk factor.

Factors in Personal Histories

At look at the personal histories of people who commit violent acts shows that risk factors are not only present at the time they commit violence, but they are also present over their lifetimes. From interviews I have done with about 150 people who committed serious violence such as murder, attempted murder, physical assault, armed robbery, rape, and child sexual abuse, I have identified three risks that are consistently present in the life stories of persons who commit violent acts. Persons who commit violent acts have poor relationships with others, have difficulty managing their emotions and behaviors, and have beliefs that hurt others. Furthermore they enjoy thinking about violence and committing it, sometimes to the point of bliss and ecstasy. I have seen these patterns over many years of talking to people who have committed serious acts of violence.

People who do well are the opposite. They have good relationships with others, regulate their emotions and behaviors in appropriately, and have beliefs that promote the well-being of others and of the self. These are protective factors. Protective factors are associated with resilience when persons have risks for poor outcomes, such as acting in antisocial ways. Persons who are resilient use these protective factors to cope with, adapt to, and overcome risks. I have seen these patterns over many years of talking to people who had risks for committing serious acts of violence and did not. The following provides detail on these three factors.

Relationships

People who have risks for violence but who do not commit violent acts have people they can talk to about personal, sensitive matters. These people can be peers or adults, inside or outside of the family or both, and with whom the at-risk person reciprocates a sense of closeness, seeks support and counsel during times of stress and fear, and freely shares painful personal issues. Typically persons who show resilience have these kinds of confidant relationships of more than two years with both peers and adults, who can be parents, siblings, peers, coaches, teachers, and parents of friends.

Supplements to talking to people they trust are journals or diaries young people keep, or other forms of verbal expression such as writing poetry or stories. Playing musical instruments, drawing, and sculpture are also avenues of emotion expression. Physical activities and recreation offer constructive ways of expressing emotions.

As they talk through issues that bother them, they feel better and they develop strategies for dealing with the difficult issues. Confidants serve many purposes such as provide comfort, validation, and opportunities to problem-solve, which involves consideration of a range of responses to issues and thinking through consequences of various responses.

In addition, individuals with risk for violent acts but who do not commit them work hard at being like the people they admire. When they admire prosocial persons, they learn through observation the value of prosocial actions.

People who develop violent behaviors are closed off from other people. They do not confide personal, painful issues to others. Instead of finding relief through talking out their issues and of identifying constructive ways of dealing with their issues, they are on their own to figure out what to do. Unfortunately, they find plenty of material that encourages them to hurt others with little thought of consequences. They become self-centered, where what matters is what they want. Other people become tools or objects to make them feel good.

People who have low risks for violence know what they are feeling, express these feelings in ways that do not harm self or others, and understand and respect how others feel. When they are confused, hurt, or angry, for example, they know this. They also know they need to do something about these emotions. Typically they talk to others about their feelings and feel better afterward. Sometimes they will do other things to help themselves feel better, such as meditate, go for a run or walk, listen to soothing music, or do something enjoyable and affirming.

They do not get drunk, beat someone up, or cut themselves. Beating someone else is obviously a violent act and could be a factor in even more dangerous forms of violence. Getting drunk or self-harm are not in themselves risks for violence toward others, but they could be factors, along with other factors, associated with potential for violence toward others. Self-destructive behaviors are of concern and can be thought of as violence toward the self, bringing their own kinds of satisfaction that are not antisocial but they are harmful.

In summary, confidant relationships lead to emotional expressiveness, which is emotional intelligence (Goleman, 1995). Emotionally expressiveness or emotional intelligence means that individuals can identify their own inner processes and express them in appropriate ways. They also connect to and have empathy for the emotions and situations of others. When individuals have emotional intelligence, they may think about doing something hurtful, but they immediately consider consequences for themselves and for others. They then think of other more constructive actions to take to reach their goals that typically are related to efforts to self-regulate or help the self feel better.

Newspaper reports describe the gunman in the Sandy Hook killings as quiet with few or no friends. He lived with his mother in a lovely home that was so far away from the road that it was difficult to see. A week before he killed the children, the teachers at the elementary school, his mother, and himself, his mother told a friend that she was having trouble reaching her son and was afraid she was losing him. A man who babysat the gunman ten years ago said the gunman's mother had given instructions never to turn his back on the boy and never to go to the bathroom in order to keep the boy in his sight. The babysitter thought these instructions were odd. Neighbors said the gunman was quiet and kept to himself and never got in trouble. This portrait of the gunman suggests that he did not talk to trusted others about sensitive, personal information. Whatever issues he had, he appears to have kept to himself.

Self-Regulation

Through close, confidant relationships with others over time, individuals develop capacities for self-regulation. Self-regulation means persons express their emotions and engage in behaviors that do not harm others or the self. Individuals with good self-regulation think about the consequences of their actions for themselves and others in the short-term and the long term. They consult with others to consider alternatives and to think through consequences. Thus, self-regulation and close personal relationships are linked not only in terms of the development of self-regulation but also in its maintenance.

Self-regulation is part of executive function, which stands for many related capacities that are composed of judgment, problem-solving, anticipation of consequences, emotion and behavioral regulation, problem solving, and following rules and directions. Problem solving involves strategies that include seeking to understand issues from multiple points of view, the consideration of various types of actions when actions are called for, and the consideration of a wide range of consequences for others and the self. When persons perform actions, they then evaluate the actions for their consequences. They continue actions that enhance others and the self, and they modify their actions to avoid negative consequences for others and the self.

People who have good self-regulation skills also engage in constructive behaviors when they are stressed. For example, to soothe themselves they may listen to music, engage in affirming self-talk, watch a funny video, go for a long walk or other enjoyable activity, and make plans for a fulfilling future. They typically talk to trusted others. They may read books related to their issues. Some seek professional counseling and therapy or join self-help groups.

People self-regulate in four general ways. One is prosocial as already described. A second in antisocial which is what I described earlier. To elaborate further, antisocial self-regulation involves individuals who harm other people as a way to regulate their emotions and make themselves feel better. They may kick dogs, drive aggressively, make derogatory comments on the internet, be verbally abusive to family members and friends, and think of raping and/or beating others. Some men go to bars and pick fights because when they do they get a high.

Raoul, 42, a man I interviewed and who was in prison for life for three murders told me

> It might have felt good at the time, but after I got busted it didn't feel good. I wasn't thinking about prison. I blocked everything out. I don't know what it is. When I think about it, there was always a couple I thought about hurting. It was always, 'I'm going to kill him. I want to kill him.' I didn't realize that prison was there. I wasn't even looking at prison. If I would have been thinking about prison, I never would have offed him. I think I would've walked away from it. I hate prison with a passion.

The gunman in the Sandy Hook obviously used antisocial methods of self-regulation. Thinking about and planning the killings probably were sources of satisfaction and shooting his way into the school and shooting little children and women also provided him with great satisfaction. He may even have enjoyed pulling the trigger while aiming the gun at himself because he knew in doing so he would escape the shame of punishment and public exposure. He only anticipated consequences he valued. He apparently got exactly what he wanted.

A third means of self-regulation is self-harm, where individuals think they will feel better if they overeat, take drugs, use alcohol, go on a shopping spree, and cut or burn themselves, among other self-destructive acts. They typically do feel better for a short time. Then they return to their usual miserable state. They get to a point where they want to feel better and once again do something that harms themselves in the long run but provides temporary relief.

More than a year before the killings, the Sandy Hook gunman burned himself with a lighter his mother told a friend. He may have done other self-destructive things, but the available information is scanty.

The fourth means of self-regulations is inappropriate behavior. Examples include not following simple rules like turn-taking in conversations, making jokes at serious occasions, humming during a quiet period when with a group, and walking around a room with no apparent goal in mind when everyone else present is engaged in a task.

The man who babysat the Sandy Hook gunman said as a boy the gunman was withdrawn and preoccupied with particular tasks. He also sometimes had tantrums that the babysitter had only seen in toddlers. These behaviors appear to be inappropriate for a ten year-old boy. He continued to be withdrawn until his death, which suggests a long-term set of inappropriate behaviors.

The Sandy Hook gunman appears not to have used prosocial means of dealing with things that bothered him, given the evidence that he kept to himself and his mother felt she was losing him. He obviously used antisocial means of dealing with issues. He also used self-destructive strategies such as burning himself. These self-destructive patterns may have been apparent for years. to keep his eye on the boy at all times, not even to take the time to go to the bathroom. His behaviors may have been inappropriate as well, such as his frequent withdrawn behaviors when in social situations.

Some newspaper reports stated that the Sandy Hook gunman had a mental disability, and used this to explain why he killed children, adults, and himself. This observation overlooks the fact that most people with mental disabilities do not harm others. They are no more likely to act out in violent ways than people who do not have mental disabilities, or mental illnesses, or brain conditions such as autism or bipolar issues. The same principles hold true for persons abused and neglected in childhood. Many believe that being abused and neglected is the reason people commit violent acts. This belief ignores the fact that most persons who have experienced abuse and neglect do not go on to be abusive and neglectful. The use of alcohol and drugs also is used to explain why people commit violence. Yet, most people who use drugs and alcohol do not commit violent acts. Other factors are at play, and the chief factor appears to be belief systems that overpower any protective factors that individuals may have.

Beliefs

Beliefs may be the central issue in the commission of violent acts. Research on persons who commit terrorist acts, feminist research, as well as the research I have done with men who commit interpersonal violence show the importance of belief systems in the perpetration of violent acts. Beliefs may be so powerful that the over-ride common sense, decency, and

21

the influences of long-term supportive relationships and otherwise prosocial ways of self-regulating. In fact, sometimes self-regulation is not an issue when people commit violent acts. They commit violence because violence serves their purposes and has nothing to do with self-regulation. This appears to be the case for Raoul, quoted earlier. This is what he said about murdering another man.

> At the time, I thought that was the right thing to do because of the life I was living and the rules of the street. He stole something from me. I felt that he had to pay for it. If I let him get away with it, that would mean other people would want to try it.

Earlier, he had called this murder "a business transaction." He also thought he would get away with it because his father used to say that people get away with the murder of black people. Raoul himself was African American.

Individuals who feel some connection to others often contact people they love before they commit violent acts. For instance, after Omar Thornton, 32, killed six people at work, he called his mother to say goodbye. He asked her to tell "everybody" he loved them. Then he shot himself. His beliefs that murders and suicide were the right things for him to do over-rode the love and potential comfort he might have received from talking to his loved ones about what was on his mind.

Other beliefs may also be at issue in Omar's case and in many others, such as the Sandy Hook gunman. Omar and almost all mass murderers are men. Beliefs about what it means to be a man may prohibit some men from discussing personal, sensitive issues. Thus, their stress builds and they seek ways of feeling better. Ideologies of violence may become their solace.

Beliefs that I have often found in my interview research with persons who have committed violent actions are of several types. Persons who commit violent actions may be getting back at others or doing unto others what they believe others have done to them, which is often the case with mass murderers. They may want to show others that you don't mess around with them. They may want to teach a lesson. They may feel depressed and thoughts of violence lift their mood. They may want to prove they've got guts. Violence may sometimes solve a problem, or at least perpetrators think so.

People who do not commit violent acts live by such values as dignity and worth of other persons and themselves. They respect the self-determination of others and their own innate right to make decisions that affect themselves. They, therefore, believe that acts that harm others are wrong. They do not believe there is justification for hurting others. They have developed a strong will not to harm others and often want to promote the well-being of others and of the self.

Other beliefs of prosocial people are the following.

- Living well is the best revenge;
- Negotiation is the way to redress wrongs, not betting back at others;
- Masculinity involves respect for women and girls, other men and boys, and the self; and
- Equates masculinity with expressing emotions directly & empathically expressiveness.

These ideas are starting points. They can be the basis of a wide range of types of actions, programs, and policies that promote individual and common good and that diminish the likelihood that persons will use violence to serve their own short-sighted ends.

Discussion

Three factors that are present in persons who do not commit violent acts: affirming relationships with others, self-regulation, and prosocial beliefs. These three factors are absent, or largely absent, in persons who do commit violent acts. No matter what pressures people experience, the tipping point toward violence occurs when persons make a decision to act on their ideologies of violence and no thoughts of dire consequences come to mind. The brother of the Sandy Hook murderer undoubtedly has had violent thoughts, but like everyone else who does not behave in harmful ways, automatic activation of thoughts of dire consequences dispelled the violent thoughts.

The Sandy Hook gunman, had no such protective processes. He thought about violence. No thoughts of consequences deterred him. He acted out his violent thoughts, took the lives of 27 people and then himself, to great long-last grief of many people and to his own great satisfaction and gratification.

Prosocial responses to stress and prosociality in general are related to capacities for emotional intelligence (Goleman, 1995), both in terms of knowing and expressing one's own emotions in appropriates ways and also connecting to and having empathy for the emotions and situations of others. No one, however, is prosocial all of the time. Even children and adolescents who actively use protective processes and demonstrate their pro-social resilience in a variety of situations over time have vulnerabilities. Coping with the effects of adversities may be life-long, although as time goes on such coping may become more automatic and the sting of the vulnerabilities may lessen. Persons with emotional intelligence actively seek ways of coping positively with things that bother them.

Some persons dig deep into the thoughts of violence. I have. I realized that these thoughts puff me up and give me momentary lift or thrill, until my protective factors kick in and consequences stop my thinking about violence. I didn't realize I have these experiences until I was years into my interview research with persons who have committee violent acts. Conversations with trusted others jogged my hidden thoughts about violence into awareness. There's something about how we function that helps us to push down thoughts we are ashamed of.

What's amazing about the prevention of violence is that so many people in so many walks of life are already making major contributions. Parents who model concern for the well-being of others and of themselves, who have affirming relationships with others, and who have good self-regulation model for their children ways of conducting themselves in prosocial ways. They also teach values such as dignity and worth of persons, social justice, and fairness to their children. Teachers, early childhood educators, social workers, people in other helping professions, people in medical fields, and elected officials who act to promote the common good are already contributing to the prevention of violence and a social contract that promotes the common good. Leaders of religious institutions dedicate their lives to promotion of individual and social good.

More, however, needs to be done. If the contributing factors are relationships, self-regulation, and belief systems, how can we as individuals and as groups acting together promote them even more than we do now? National and even international campaigns to help adults become better at connecting with young people might be helpful. The advantages of talking to people about what's troubling you can also become part of this campaign. Efforts can be at the national, regional, state-wide, and local levels by people from all walks of life.

Campaigns of this sort to educate people about how to cope with issues that bother them and about the dangers of taking on beliefs that violence is the answer could also have benefits.

I hope this article shows that two brothers, who have the same parents, who grew up in the same family, and who lived in the same neighborhoods could have different outcomes. Like the Sandy Hook gunman, the Unabomber, who killed three people and wounded many others had a law-abiding brother who turned him in. The Unabomber's brother ran a shelter for runaway youth who had been abused and neglected.

One brother dealt with issues that troubled him in prosocial ways, had affirming relationships with others, and reject beliefs about violence and espoused prosocial beliefs. Each of us individually and collectively have responsibilities to promote the common good and to protect others and ourselves from harm. Thinking in terms of these three factors may clarify goals and strategies and lead to informed violence prevention efforts.

References

14 dead, 50 wounded in shooting at Colorado theater, police chief says (2012). CNN US, July 20. http://articles.cnn.com/2012-07-20/us/us_colorado-theater-shooting_1_gunshot-wounds-gunman-theater

Boroff, David (2012). Adam Lanza's babysitter Ryan Kraft stunned by mass murder at Sandy Hook Elementary School. *New York Daily News*, December 17. http://www.nydailynews.com/news/national/adam-lanza-babysitter-stunned-sandy-hook-tragedy-article-1.1221855

Connecticut shooting horror (2010). New York Post. August 4. http://www.nypost.com/f/mobile/news/local/connecticut_shooting_horror_mjGpPhDo2vxzvfS9RVkmwM

Buber, Martin (1937/2004). *I and thou.* London: Continuum.

Fromm, Erich (1956/2008). *The art of loving.* New York: Continuum.

Gilgun, Jane F. (2012). *The logic of murderous rampages and other essays on violence.* Amazon.

Gilgun, Jane F. (2011). *Child sexual abuse: From harsh realities to hope.* Amazon, Kindle, & Nook.

Gilgun, Jane F. (2010). Evil feels good: Think before you action. Chapter in present book. http://www.amazon.com/s/ref=nb_sb_noss?url=search-alias%3Daps&field-keywords=Jane+Gilgun+evil+feels+good: Think before you act.

Gilgun, Jane F. (2011). Original sin is not original, but goodness is. http://www.scribd.com/doc/49564877/Original-Sin-is-Not-Original-Goodness-is

Gilgun, Jane F. (2010). Nujood Ali, 10, divorces 30 year-old husband. http://www.amazon.com/s/ref=nb_sb_noss?url=search-alias%3Daps&field-keywords=Jane+Gilgun+Nujood

Gilgun, Jane F. (2010). Reflections on 25 years of research on violence. *Reflections: Narratives of Professional Helping,* 16(4), 50-59.

Gilgun, Jane F. (2008). Lived experience, reflexivity, and research on perpetrators of interpersonal violence. *Qualitative Social Work, 7(2),* 181-197.

Goleman, Daniel. (1996). *Emotional intelligence: Why it can matter more than IQ.* New York: Barnes and Noble.

Lysiak, Matthew, Kerry Wills, & Stephen Rex Brown (2012). EXCLUSIVE: Nancy Lanza feared son, Adam, was "getting worse;" told friend 'he was burning himself with a lighter' and that she was "losing him. *New York Daily News*, December 18. http://www.nydailynews.com/news/national/nancy-lanza-feared-son-adam-worse-article-1.1221505

Sharma, Alankaar & Jane F. Gilgun (2008). What perpetrators say about child sexual abuse. *Indian Journal of Social Work, 69(3),* 321-338.

4

On Being Happy:
Three Ideas

Most people want to be happy. Unhappy people may be unhappy in their own ways, but happy people are similar to each other. Happy people have good relationships with others, manage their emotions well, and have beliefs that promote their own well-being and the well-being of others. The purpose of this brief article is to show how these three ideas lead to happiness.

Building Relationships

Human beings throughout history have recognized the importance of relationships and have acted that way much of the time. Through relationships with others we build families and communities. We engage in commerce—that is, the creation, buying, and selling of food, goods, and services that are necessary to sustain life. When we have good relationships with others, we feel good. We treat others well. We are creative and relaxed.

When something goes wrong in important relationships, we are sad, stressed, and angry. Happy people seek to repair breaks in relationships.

Research has shown consistently that the chief quality in good relationships is not the absence of conflict but capacities to repair breakdowns in relationships.

Managing Emotions

Managing emotions means that we have capacities to regulate our emotions. Much of the time, our emotions are on an even keel. No matter how stable we think our emotions are, there are times when we become frustrated, angry, or sad, among other emotions. What we do when we feel these strong emotions leads to happiness or unhappiness. Happy people know how to manage or regulate their emotions. They allow themselves to feel these emotions. They talk to other people about their

27

emotions. They are willing to deal with their emotions constructively. They do not express their emotions destructively.

Happy people self-regulate, by doing talking to others, vigorous exercise, meditate, dance, go for a run or walk, swim, engage in an enjoyable activity, or anything else that soothes difficult emotions. Happy people do not take their emotions out on others. They do not do things that hurt themselves. They know what they feel. They can name their emotions. They admit what they feel. They deal directly and constructively with their emotions.

No one is constructive 100% of the time. When generally happy people do things that hurt themselves and others, these actions usually are not deeply harmful and the effects are repairable. Having too much to drink can be harmful, but easily correctable. Eating too much to self-soothe can be harmful, but correctable. Being irritable hurts others but is repairable. Happy people recognize quickly when they are out of line. Sometimes others have to tell them. When others do this, they realize that they are out of line. They take corrective actions. They seek to repair harms.

Sometimes frustrations lead to problem-solving. Parents and teachers who simply don't know what to do about a family or classroom issue do problem-solving. They seek out a variety of people to get a variety of points of view. They may take special training. They consider alternatives and then make decisions about how to respond. When they do respond they observe what happens. If things turn out well, they continue to perform those actions. If they find some things don't work and some do, they seek constructive ways to deal with issues where their actions weren't helpful.

Challenge Belief Systems

Happy people have balanced ideas of who they are, what they are entitled to, and what they can do to get what they want. Happy people negotiate for what they want. They balance what they want with what other people want. They actively seek to understand what other people want. They adjust their own wants to what others want.

Having accurate ideas of who they are means that they don't think they are entitled to what they want regardless of what others want. They also don't think of themselves as worthless. They also don't swing between entitlement and worthlessness.

Happy people believe they have a right to be respected, to make their own decisions, and have dignity and worth. When they feel disrespected. Controlled, or demeaned, they speak up assertively. They are not aggressive about it.

Happy people believe that others have a right to be respected, to make their own decision, and have dignity and worth. They do nothing to infringe on the rights of others. If they are parents, teachers, bosses, or others who have power over others, they recognize the power they have and allow others to have as much power as if feasible, as much freedom of choice as possible, and as much dignity and worth as possible. They set fair rules and provide resources so that they persons over whom they have power have what they need to be able to follow the rules.

Happy people do not abuse their power or take advantage of the power they have over others. They are just and caring in their dealings with others.

Happy people do not have beliefs that lead them to refuse to consider the rights of others, including the rights of others to make their own decisions within reasonable boundaries.

Happy people want others to challenge their beliefs when beliefs lead to actions that hurt other people or themselves.

Happy people operate on the principles of fairness and caring for others.

Discussion

Abraham Lincoln said people are as happy as they make up their minds to be. This means that to be happy can take a lot of effort and discipline. Rarely are happy people happy by sitting around. Lincoln himself had many tragedies in his life, but he use his strong will to focus on what was important to him.

Some people have genetic predispositions to depression. Sometimes these predispositions are so powerful that they overcome the protective factors of relationships, self-regulation, and prosocial beliefs. Yet, most people with depression do not harm others, but they are at risk to harm themselves. Some cope with their depression in a variety of ways, which mean they regulate their emotions, including their depressive emotions, maintain confidant relationships with others, and focus on prosocial beliefs. They seek help when they have thoughts of being self-destructive.

Therefore, the three factors related to happiness still hold for persons with depression if they use prosocial means of coping. If they do not, their typical means of coping is self-injurious, including the use of drugs and alcohol, risky behaviors, and addictions of various sorts.

Some people with depression harm others. The chances are good that when they do, they have detached from others, obviously have let go of the will to regulate themselves prosocially, and have focuses on self-destructive beliefs.

Happiness is complicated. We pursue happiness through trusting relationships, self-regulation, and prosocial beliefs. Unattended traumas and genetic predispositions to depression complicate the pursuit of happiness. With help from friends and family in whom we confide and with a will to seek happiness, even persons who have difficult life circumstances can hope for happier days.

5

Detecting
the Potential for Violence

When anyone threatens to commit violence, the threats must be taken seriously. It's important to immediately assess for positives in the lives of individuals who make threats. People, young or old, male and female, sometimes make threats in the heat of the moment. Later, they want to take the threats back. They have so many positive factors in their lives that they are at low risk to harm others. In addition, they have few if any other risk factors for being violent.

Persons at low risk do not believe that violence is a means of getting what they want and what they want does not place unreasonable demands on others. They also are emotionally expressive. This means they can identify a wide range of emotions in themselves and express them in ways that do not harm others or themselves. They can identify the emotions of others and empathize with them. In other words, they experience in themselves how others are feeling and, in response, modify their behaviors in positive ways.

Other times, danger is at hand. The chief risk factors are a sense of being entitled to their version of respect and deference and their beliefs that violence is a way to get respect and to get other things that they think they are entitled to.

Terrorism and mass murders often rests upon beliefs that individuals are entitled to murder innocent children, women, and men for the sake of their beliefs.

Persons who have to decide about the levels of risk for violent behaviors must look at a wide range of factors. The following is a framework for assessing the potential for violence. The framework covers five areas:

1) precipitating events,

2) patterns of direct statements,

31

3) circumstances that increase the likelihood of violence,

4) signs of cumulative stress, and

5) indicators of lowered risks for violence.

I elaborate on each of these areas in this chapter. First, I discuss ways to approach people with signs of risks

What to Do

When young people and adults have any of this signs of risk, an approach of choice is to spend time with these persons. Get to know them. Do things with them that they enjoy. Get them involved in activities with other people, but make sure knowledgeable adults supervise these activities. Sometimes forming positive relationships can change how people thoughts about harming others. Forming these relationships take time, effort, and commitment. Often people with these risks require long-term, loving and supportive relationships that include group work, individual therapy, recreational therapy, supervised volunteer activities, engagement in educational settings, and any activity that builds up their desires to be prosocial.

The key elements to lowering risks for violence are

- Relationships with positive people;

- Opportunities to explore their beliefs and the consequences of their beliefs; and

- Opportunities to explore alternatives to violence.

Telling people to change their ways, giving advice, and talking without genuine, engaged give and take are approaches that adults often use. These approaches do not work. Nor do isolating people or kicking them out of schools, social clubs, or any setting. This only moves the problem to another setting.

The first step in prevention is to engage persons in genuine relationships where trust, mutuality, and positive regard are present. When persons have positive relationships, the stage is set for the development of emotional expressiveness and for modifying beliefs that lead to violence.

Emotional expressiveness is, along with pro-social beliefs, the single most important factor in overcoming risks for violence. Emotional expressiveness is a capacity to identity and express a wide range of emotions in appropriate ways; that is, in ways that don't harm self and others but promote the well-being of self and others or at least are neutral in their effects.

Persons with lowered risk for violence share personal, painful experiences and express a wide range of emotions with at least one other person and finds that doing so helps them to feel better and to approach challenges in new ways, ways that do not harm themselves or others.

Lowered risk for violence is also associated with capacities not only to understand the consequences of violence but also to take actions to avoid these consequences.

Precipitating Events

When individuals commit violent acts, there often but not always is a precipitating event. Examples include Major Nidal Hasan, the Army psychiatrist who is accused of killing 13 people and wounding dozens of others at Ford Hood, Texas, USA, in November 2009. Major Hasan believed he was about to be deployed to Iraq or Afghanistan, and he did not want to go. Another is Kip Kinkel, who killed his parents and two classmates, and wounded 22 others. He told a classmate the day before the killings that he wanted to get back at the people who had expelled him from school that day. He was expelled for having a loaded pistol in his locker. Andrew Golden, 13, who murdered a teacher and classmates in Jonesboro, AK, had been rejected by a girl on whom he had a crush.

According to an accomplice to five of his murders, Genildo Ferreira de Franca, a Brazilian who killed 15 people in 1997, laughed as if the devil possessed him after each murder. He had experienced two precipitating events: his young son had died and his father-in-law spread rumors that Franca was gay. Franca's mother said, "But that was not true," she said, "My son was a womanizer."

Sometimes there is no known precipitating event. Thomas Hamilton, who murdered 16 young children and their teacher, had no known precipitators, but instead appeared to have seethed in rage for more than 20 years on slights and rejections he'd experienced. In particular, he was enraged at being dropped Boy Scout leader all those years ago. This was a man the children in his village in Scotland called "Mr. Creepy" for his voyeuristic interest in boys.

Patterns of Direct Statements

Direct statements about committing violence are red flags. When persons have made statements more than once, to several different people, at different times, and in different contexts (e.g., home, schoolyard, classroom, neighborhood, workplace, another social setting), the danger is increased. Sometimes they are just blowing off steam and do not have a pattern of making violent threats. Such persons are unlikely to be at risk, as stated in the introduction, but to make such judgments, social workers and others who do assessments must look at the overall patterns of positive behaviors and beliefs and pro-violence behaviors and beliefs.

Verbal statements

Verbal statements include talking about harming/killing others, idolizing violent heroes, and providing specific details of how the violence will take place, including who the intended victims are, and when and where the violent events are to take place. These statements often are made gleefully, as if the person is enjoying thinking of harming, mutilating, and killing others.

Written statements

Writing poems and stories about killing people could be warning signs in combination with other indicators. The more often the person does this and the variety of places in which such writings are shared may increase the likelihood of violence. Joy and glee in anticipating this violence are major red flags.

Circumstances that Increase
the Likelihood of Violence

The likelihood of committing violence increases when other factors are present. The following is a list of factors identified in the lives of people who commit violent acts. The more factors that are present, the higher the likelihood of violence.

Preoccupation with violence

- Spending hours a day playing violent videos, listening to violent music, playing violent games, reading about violence, writing about violence

- Beliefs that violence is the means of choice to get what you want, to assert manhood, to redress wrongs, and to exact vengeance.

- Enjoyment of these violent activities, including enjoyment of thinking about harming others

- Collecting weapons

- Not understanding that violence hurts other people permanently

- Seeing violence as a way of demonstrating manhood and "guts"

34

Means to commit the violence

- Access to weapons
- A history of fascination with weapons

Patterns of bullying and being bullied

- A history of being bullied
- Feeling picked on and full of resentment about being bullied
- A history of bullying others

Note: most children who are bullied feel hurt and do not fantasize about and make plans to hurt others. Being bullied by itself is not sufficient to act out violently. There must be other risk facts that operate as well and few if any factors that diminish the risk for violence.

Psychological vulnerability

- Perceptions of self as weak and powerless
- Fantasies about hurting others
- "Attachments" to violent others
- Wanting to please violent others to the point where own moral compass is lost

Note: Many people are psychologically vulnerable, but they do not commit violence. Psychological vulnerability as defined here includes dangerous ways of coping with vulnerability. Most people who experience vulnerability deal with these issues constructively and do not seek to harm others.

Part of a group preoccupied with violence

- The group has violent initiation rites
- The group has one or more leader who advocates violence
- The group has a set of core beliefs that bind members together; most of these beliefs advocate violence to further the mission of the group
- Violence within the group is a means of showing that you've got guts
- Leaders of the group manipulate one or more members; the members must susceptible to manipulation may be at highest risk to act out in violent ways.

Violence in the families of origin

This violence includes wife beating and rape, physical, sexual, and emotional abuse, and witnessing or being the target of such violence. Family practices can normalize violent behaviors so that it is natural for children growing up in these families.

Patterns of glorifying violence

Many people glorify violence as a mark of manhood. Glorifying means that members of peer groups or families congratulate the violent persons and give them respect and honor. Violence-prone persons may actively seek to spend time with others who also glorify violence.

Entitlement

Some people believe they are entitled to get what they want when they want. They push this belief to such an extent that they are willing to use whatever it takes, including violence, to get what they want.

Each additional factor increases the potential for violence.

Indirect Indicators:
Signs of Cumulative Stress

Indirect indicators increase the likelihood of persons acting out violently, but by themselves they are indicators of serious issues that indicate the persons need intervention. If direct communication discussed earlier is not present, the likelihood of violence is diminished. If direct communication of violence and these signs of cumulative stress are present, then the likelihood of violence is increased.

Emotionally closed

An inability to share personal and private hurts, rejections, abandonments, and a sense of failure can increase risk for violence in persons who have other risks. Often persons who are emotionally closed have distanced themselves from their emotions and are unaware of how their inner states may be affecting them.

Shame and feeling defective

A sense of self as powerless and unworthy can lead to a sense of shame and feeling defective.

Unshared anger and grief

Unshared anger and grief may lead to a sense of the self as bad and deserving of bad things. The root meaning of anger is grief.

Anti-social behaviors

These behaviors include vandalism, shoplifting, stealing, and beating others up.

Often related to psychological stress and vulnerability, sometimes these crimes could result from a sense of entitlement, meaning these persons are destructive because they can get away with it and feel they have a right to behave in these ways.

Chemical abuse

Risks for violence include misuse of alcohol, drug use, use of inhalants, and sniffing glue. If individuals do not have capacities to express their emotions appropriately, they may use chemicals as a way of providing emotional release and comfort.

Self-injurious behaviors

These behaviors include cutting, eating problems, suicide attempts, talk of suicide.

Other Signs of Cumulative Stress

There are many signs of cumulative stress that merit attention, such as chronic behavioral maladaption, conduct disorders, chronic angry outbursts, psychosomatic disorders, dissociative reactions, phobias, depressive/suicidal thinking, social isolation, sleep disorders, night terrors, and sleep walking.

Many persons have these signs of cumulative stress but are not at risk to act out violently. They do not show patterns of making direct and indirect statements about their intentions to commit violence. They do not believe that they can do whatever they want, and they do not dream about hurting others to make themselves feel better.

Indicators of Lowered Risk

The following factors diminish the likelihood that individuals will act out verbal threats. The more negative factors that a person has, however, and the fewer positive factors, such as those listed below, the more likely it is that violence will take place.

Emotional expressiveness

This is the most important indicator of emotional health. Persons with lowered risk for violence share personal, painful experiences and express a wide range of emotions with at least one other person and finds that doing so helps them to feel better and to approach challenges in new ways, ways that do not harm themselves or others.

Automatic rejection of violent thoughts

Persons with lowered risk for violence may have violent thoughts from time to time, but when these thoughts arise they immediately think of the damage that such behaviors would cause. They immediately realize that others would be hurt, and, in the long run, they would be hurt by their own guilt and remorse and then hurt by other consequences such as public shame, arrests, court appearances, and possible jail time or prison.

Management of stress prosocially

Persons with lowered risks for violence choose prosocial ways of dealing with anger, range, frustration, and other negative emotions. They may talk to others about these strong feelings, or use other prosocial means, such as journaling, self-talk, meditation, yoga, vigorous exercise, and seek out prosocial, positive person.

Empathy for others

Connecting to others on both emotional and cognitive levels and having respect for others is an important indicator of emotional health. Sometimes persons with lowered risk for violence may not feel much empathy for others, but they also do nothing that would harm others.

Good interpersonal skills

Individuals with good interpersonal skills have lowered risks for violence. These skills include sharing personal issues with others, negotiating for what they want, knowing how to admit wrong-doing, taking responsibility for hurtful behaviors, and making amends for hurtful behaviors.

Spends time with friends who are pro-social

Admiring and emulating pro-social friends is a hopeful sign that persons are functioning well. Feeling accepted by pro-social friends with whom they've shared their most personal secrets is a strong indicator of emotional health.

Sense of humor

This is very important, indicating abilities to take a "long" view of present difficulties and to find humor in difficult situations. The humor, however, cannot be sadistic, at the expense of others.

Optimistic about the future

Persons with low risk for violence have clear plans for achieving dreams for the future, have abilities that match plans, learn about possibilities for the future from successful people, and show persistence when circumstances seem to block plans for future. Adults, too, show an optimism about their work, their leisure, and their personal relationships.

Capacities for emotional expressiveness

Persons who have lowered risks for violence have at least one confidant, with whom another person

Has a close relationship with at least one parent

While a child and adolescent, having a pro-social parent, grandparent, sibling, or other family member to whom the person is close is important. Indicators of closeness include sharing personal, private, and painful life events with the adult and finding that this helps; parental interest in the person's activities and encouragement in several areas, such as emotional expressiveness, school work if in school, planning for the future, and work life, if an adult.

Close relationships with adults other than parents

Sometimes relationships within families are not very good, but during childhood and adolescence, individuals can have good relationships with adults outside of the family. Having good relationships within families and with persons outside of families is the best possible combination. Adults with close personal relationships characterized by mutuality and reciprocity in the exchange of personal and private experiences and emotions have a lowered risk for acting out violently. These relationships are associated with lowered risk for violence when they are long-term, and not involving sporadic contact with a variety of persons, as can often be the case when children and youth are in out-of-home care.

Willingness to negotiate

Well functioning persons negotiate for what they want. They don't feel entitled. They don't just take what they want regardless of what affected others might want. They negotiate and work for what they want.

Rejection of ideologies of entitlement

Children and adults at lower risk for acting in violent ways have pro-social beliefs and do not believe that they are entitled to force, bully, or harm others to get what they believe they are supposed to have. If other people belittle them or do not like them, they may feel hurt and angry, but they deal with their hurt and anger in ways that do not hurt others. They do not believe that in order to assert their dignity and worth they have to get back at others by hurting them.

Summary

In detecting the potential for violence, positive factors must be looked for as well as the negative factors. When the negatives outweigh the positives, the situation is serious. One or two negative factors in combination with many positives might indicate individuals who are blowing off steam and are not threats. Beliefs about entitlement and the rightness of taking what you want or redressing perceived wrongs through violent means are major red flags that can over-ride many seemingly positive factors in individual lives.

Violence is not an isolated incident. It arises from uncaring non-responsive environments that espouse violence as means to ends. Each act of violence inflicts life-long harm on survivors and on the fabric of families and communities. Dealing forthrightly with individuals who have potential for violence will go a long way toward promoting personal, familial, and community safety. In many cases, persons with potential for violence want to stopped. They would trade in their violent fantasies for a secure place in social groups and to feel part of loving and accepting families and communities. Some others are hardened into their beliefs that violence solves their problems and asserts their place in the world as in charge and entitled to their ideas of respect and deference.

Social workers have major roles to play in detecting the potential for violence. We often are the first professionals called upon when danger is present. We can also contribute to prevention efforts through psychoeducation and through helping to develop policies and procedures that can distinguish between persons with a high risk for violence and those with lowered risks.

The social work value of social justice commits us to promote family and community safety by containing persons who are at serious risk and to deal fairly with persons who may have a single "risk" for violence but who also have substantial indicators that they have lowered risks.

The implications of social justice directs social workers and other human service professionals to find the strengths in at-risk children, youth, and adults and to develop guidelines for "reclaiming" them and helping them find places in loving and accepting families and communities where they can contain their violent thoughts and learn constructive ways of dealing with major stressors (Brendtro, Brokenleg, & Van Brockern, 1990; Gilgun, 2002).

Note

Parts of this article were published in a social work journal. This is the citation.

Gilgun, Jane F. (2002). Social work and the assessment of the potential for violence. In Tan Ngoh Tiong & Imelda Dodds (Eds.), *Social work around the world II* (pp. 58-74). Berne, Switzerland: International Federation of Social Workers.

References

Brendtro, Larry. K., Martin Brokenleg & Steve Van Bockern (1990). *Reclaiming youth at risk: Our hope for the future.* Bloomington, IN: National Educational Service.

Frazer, Mark W. (Ed.) (1997). *Risk and resilience in childhood: An ecological perspective.* Washington, D.C.: NASW Press.

Gilgun, Jane F. (2002). Completing the circle: American Indian Medicine Wheels and the promotion of resilience in children and youth in care. *Journal of Human Behavior and the Social Environment, 6(2),* 65-84.

Gilgun, Jane F. (1999a). CASPARS: Clinical Assessment Instruments that measure strengths and risks in children and families. In Martin C. Calder (Ed.*), Working with young people who sexually abuse: New pieces of the jigsaw puzzle.* Dorset, England: Russell House.

Gilgun, Jane F. (1999b). CASPARS: New tools for assessing client risks and strengths. *Families in Society, 80,* 450-459. Tools available at http://ssw.che.umn.edu/faculty/jgilgun.htm

Gilgun, Jane F. (1999c). Fingernails painted red: A feminist, semiotic analysis of "hot" text, *Qualitative Inquiry, 5,* 181-207.

Gilgun, Jane F. (1999d). Mapping resilience as process among adults maltreated in childhood. In Hamilton I. McCubbin, Elizabeth A. Thompson, Anne I. Thompson, & Jo A. Futrell (Eds.), *The dynamics of resilient families.* (pp. 41-70*).* Thousand Oaks, CA: Sage.

Gilgun, Jane F. (1996a). Human development and adversity in ecological perspective, Part 2: Three patterns. *Families in Society, 77,* 459-576.

Gilgun, Jane F. (1996b). Human development and adversity in ecological perspective: Part 1: A conceptual framework. *Families in Society, 77,* 395-402.

Gilgun, Jane F. (1995). We shared something special: The moral discourse of incest perpetrators. *Journal of Marriage and the Family, 57,* 265-281.

Gilgun, Jane F. (1994a). A case for case studies in social work research. *Social Work, 39,* 371-380.

Gilgun, Jane F. (1994b). Avengers, conquerors, playmates, and lovers: A continuum of roles played by perpetrators of child sexual abuse. *Families in Society, 75,* 467-480.

Gilgun, Jane F. (1994c). Freedom of choice and research interviewing in child sexual abuse. In Beulah G. Compton & Burt Galaway, *Social work processes* (5th ed.) (pp. 358-368). Chicago: Dorsey.

Gilgun, Jane F. (1992). Hypothesis generation in social work research. *Journal of Social Service Research, 15,* 113-135.

Gilgun, Jane F. (1991). Resilience and the intergenerational transmission of child sexual abuse. In Michael Q. Patton (Ed.), *Family sexual abuse: Frontline research and evaluation* (pp. 93-105). Newbury Park, CA: Sage.

Gilgun, Jane F. (1990). Factors mediating the effects of childhood maltreatment. In Mic Hunter (Ed.), *The sexually abused male: Prevalence, impact, and treatment* (pp. 177-190). Lexington, MA: Lexington Books.

Gilgun, Jane F. (1988a). Decision-making in interdisciplinary treatment teams. *Child Abuse & Neglect, 12,* 231-239.

Gilgun, Jane F. (1988b). Self-centeredness and the adult male perpetrator of child sexual abuse. *Contemporary Family Therapy, 10,* 216-234.

Gilgun, Jane F. (1988c). Why children don't tell: Fear of separation and loss and the disclosure of child sexual abuse. *New Designs in Youth Development, 8,* 16-20.

Gilgun, Jane F. (1986). Sexually abused girls' knowledge of sexual abuse and sexuality. *Journal of Interpersonal Violence, 1,* 209-225.

Gilgun, Jane F. (1986). The adolescent sex offender and the juvenile justice system in Minnesota. In Hans J. Kerner, Burt Galaway, & H. Janssen (Eds.), *European and North-American juvenile justice systems.* Munich: Schriftenreihe der Deutschen Vereinigung fur Jugendgerichte und Jugendgerichtschilfen.

Gilgun, Jane F., & Laura McLeod (1999). Gendering violence. *Studies in Symbolic Interactionism, 22,* 167-193.

Gilgun, Jane F., & Elizabeth Reiser. (1990). Sexual identity development among men sexually abused in childhood. *Families in Society, 71,* 515-523.

Gilgun, Jane F. & Teresa M. Connor (1990). Isolation and the adult male perpetrator of child sexual abuse. In Anne L. Horton, Barry L. Johnson, Lynn M. Roundy, & Doran Williams (Eds.), *The incest perpetrator: The family member no one wants to treat* (pp. 74-87). Newbury Park, CA: Sage.

Gilgun, Jane F., & Teresa M. Connor. (1989). How perpetrators view child sexual abuse. *Social Work, 34,* 349-351.

Gilgun, Jane F. & Sol Gordon (l985). Sex education and the prevention of child sexual abuse. *Journal of Sex Education and Therapy, 11,* 46-52.

Gilgun, Jane F. Christian Klein, & Kay Pranis. (2000). The significance of resources in models of risk, *Journal of Interpersonal Violence, 14,* 627-646.

Gilgun, Jane F., Susan Keskinen, Danette Jones Marti, & Kay Rice. (1999). Clinical applications of the CASPARS instruments: Boys who act out sexually. *Families in Society, 80,* 629-641.

Gilligan, R. (1999). Enhancing the resilience of children and young people in public care by mentoring their talents and interests. *Child and Family Social Work, 4(3),* 187-196.

Jordan, Bill (1978). A comment on "theory and practice in social work." *British Journal of Social Work, 8(11),* 23-25.

Masten, Ann. S., & J. Douglas Coatsworth (1998). The development of competence in favorable and unfavorable environments: Lessons from research on successful children. *American Psychologist, 53,* 205-220.

Masten, Ann S. & Margaret O' Dougherty Wright (1998). Cumulative risk and protection models of child maltreatment. *Journal of Aggression, and Trauma, 2(1),* 7-30.

Parton, Nigel (2000). Some thoughts on the relationship between theory and practice in and for social work. *British Journal of Social Work, 30(4),* 449-463.

Saleebey, Dennis (2002). *The strengths perspective in social work practice* (3rd ed.). Boston: Allyn and Bacon.

Shields, Ann & Dante Cicchetti (1998). Reactive aggression among maltreated children: The contributions of attention and emotion dysregulation. *Journal of Clinical Child Psychology, 27,* 381-395.

Werner, Emme E., & Ruth S. Smith (l992). *Overcoming the odds: High risk children from birth to adulthood.* Ithaca, N.Y.: Cornell University Press.

6

An Open Letter
to the Boston Marathon Bomber

I wrote this letter to the bombers the day before their identities were known. I based what I said on my knowledge of other cases that are similar. I knew from previous study that people who do these terrible things typically enjoy themselves, enjoy the planning, and have beliefs that lead them to do terrible harm. They draw up beliefs that many people have and they experience a sense of solidarity with others who believe as they do. They are heroes in their own eyes.

This is what I'd like to say to the Boston bomber(s).

Are you happy now? You've killed an 8 year-old boy, and two graduate students. You blasted the leg off the boy's little sister and seriously injured their mother. The surviving family members are in shock. You've injured almost 200 children and adults. You've traumatized the eyewitnesses, family members, and everyone there. You've traumatized a nation. The world is thinking about you, what you did. You. Is that what you will write home about? Will you sit with your mother in the kitchen over tea and tell her what a good boy you've been? Will she say you're the man?

Where is the glee of anticipation now? Where is the joy you felt as you put the bombs together and dropped them off where the maximum number of children and their parents and other people would be killed, injured, and traumatized? Were you getting back at innocent people for acts that the US government has perpetrated somewhere else in the world?

Turn yourself in. Admit what you did. You did something wrong. You did something cowardly. Now show that you are a man and stand up for what you believe. Is it too much to hope that you now know what you did is wrong? That you want forgiveness? That you want to make up for what you did? Turn yourself in.

Afterword: A World-Wide Conspiracy of Hatred

I wrote this article on 18 April 2013, the day before the identities of two suspects were known. The suspects are brothers, ages 19 and 26. The older man died in a shootout. Causes of death were multiple. They included gunshot wounds, the possible explosion of a vest loaded with explosives, and being run over by his younger brother when the brother escaped the shootout in a hijacked car.

When the younger brother was caught, he said he and his brother were fighting back against the US for their involvement in wars with Afghanistan and Iraq. He did not explain how killing an 8 year-old boy, two young people, a police officer sitting in his car, and wounding more than 200 other people at a joyful public event get back at the US for war policies.

The day after the bombings, the younger man called his uncle and asked him for forgiveness. This is the uncle's statement.

> "I can't believe this what happened. It's not possible." He stated that Tamerlan, who he has not spoken with in years, called him yesterday to ask forgiveness. "Yesterday he called me and said forgive me."

The uncle asked reporters to go to his brother's house. The second uncle of the suspects said he and his family had had no contact with his nephews for several years for personal reasons that he did not disclose. He shared his thoughts about the brothers' motivation.

> What do I think provoked this? Being losers. Hatred to those who are able to settle themselves. These are the only reasons I can imagine. Anything else with religion, Islam is a fraud, a fake.

This second uncle has a point. The brothers probably had personal troubles that are factors in the bombings. News reports have circulated that the older brother was on track for a successful boxing career, but when the boxing association changed the rules that said only US citizens can participate, the older brother was ineligible. He was a legal resident and not a US citizen. He was refused citizenship because authorities thought he had ties to terrorists and that he had a felony charge for hitting his wife.

The younger brother was a US citizen because his record was clear. Many think the older brother influenced the younger brother who looked up to him. The brothers may have hated people in the US whom they saw as successful. It is likely that they turned the emotions associated with their troubles into hatred for U.S. policies. At least the older brother did, and the younger brother bought into the logic of hatred.

Law enforcement said there was no conspiracy involved in the bombings, but there was. The conspiracy is a world-wide web of hatred toward the U.S. and beliefs about what to do with the hatred. The hatred grows from perceptions of the U.S. as imperialists in our involvement in wars in the Middle East. The hatred gets translated for some into acts of violence against little kids, graduate students, and many others who have nothing to do with U.S. policy.

References

Associated Press (2013). Stories of casualties in Boston Marathon bombing. Boston Herald. April 18. http://bostonherald.com/news_opinion/local_coverage/2013/04/stories_of_casualties_in_boston_marathon_bombing Retrieved April 18, 2013.

Friedman, Thomas L. (2013). Judgment not included. *New York Times*, 29 April. http://www.nytimes.com/2013/04/28/opinion/sunday/friedman-judgment-not-included.html?ref=thomaslfriedman&_r=0

Gilgun, Jane F. (2013). *The logic of murderous rampages and other essays on violence and its prevention* (2nd ed.). http://www.amazon.com/Murderous-Rampages-Violence-Prevention-ebook/dp/B00AYPR18A/ref=sr_1_1?s=digital-text&ie=UTF8&qid=1366292206&sr=1-1&keywords=logic+of+murderous+rampages

Video: Boston Bombers' uncle asks forgiveness (2013). *Washington Times*, 19 April 2013 http://communities.washingtontimes.com/neighborhood/citizen-warrior/2013/apr/19/boston-bombers-uncle-asks-forgiveness-surrender/

7

Resilience is Relational

Resilience is an important concept in social work, education, psychology, nursing, medicine and other helping professions. In this article, I show that resilience is linked to attachment relationships, to trauma and other adversities, and to beliefs and expectations. Resilience is a term that stands for coping with, adapting to, and overcoming adversities and other stressors.

Resilience is a relational process. How well individuals handle adversities and everyday stress depends upon the inner working models (IWS) or schemas that are embedded in brain circuits. IWMs or schemas are mental maps that are composed of beliefs and expectations about the self, others, and how the world works. In general, resilience is defined as capacities for coping with, adapting to, or overcoming adversities or other major stressors.

We know who we are through our interactions with others. When we have secure attachment relationships, we have a sense of ourselves as good and worthy of respect, and we also view others as good and worthy of respect until they give us reasons to believe otherwise. Securely attached persons also recognize injustice whether against others or themselves and have over time developed skills for dealing with unjust situations.

People who as infants and over their life courses have had secure attachments have predominantly positive IWMs. This means they have positive beliefs and expectations about themselves, others, and how the world works. When they have setbacks, they respond in pro-social ways and seek to solve problems constructively, often through consultation with pro-social others.

Persons are only predominantly securely attached because no one has perfectly secure attachments. We each have experienced at least brief moments on insensitive, non-responsive care that gets encoded in schemas.

Thus, everyone has self-doubts, fears, mistrust, and negative self-appraisals of self-others and how the world works. People with longer-term experiences of insensitive, non-responsive care have larger doses of self-doubt, fears, mistrust, and negative self-appraisals. They are said to have predominantly insecure styles of attachment, and they are at risk to solve problems in anti-social, self-destructive, or dissociative ways.

Not all IWMs develop through relationships, however. Some appear to develop through observation, direct instruction, or through the mass media. However developed, persons who have histories of predominantly secure attachments are more likely to be flexible and open-minded in their thinking while those with histories of predominantly insecure attachments may have a harder time with open-mindedness and flexibility.

IWMs or schemas activate themselves continually throughout the day as we perform everyday tasks and appraise everyday situations. Almost all of these activations are automatic, such as the many schemas in operation as we wake up in the morning, get out of bed, and do whatever comes next. If we had to think about every little thing we do, it would take us a much longer time to get into the kitchen for breakfast.

Our experiences are encoded in brain circuits, and they become part of our IWMs. Thus, the brain is continually reshaping itself, almost always in terms of making new neural connections. The formation of new neurons is rare. Neurons are the cells of the brain. The brain changes as the neurons develop new connectors called dendrites that meet at the synapses which are the areas of connection between dendrites of neurons.

When individuals are confronted with stress, several different IWMs may activate themselves in response. Reminders of trauma may trigger stress reactions, some quite strong. Reminders of pleasant experiences will produce happiness or other positive emotional states.

IWMs are considered maps because the experiences, emotions, and beliefs they encode compose processes that take place over time, just as traveling from one place to another takes place over time. The processes of IWMs have several inter-related parts. When traumatic memories come into awareness, the process is as follows.

- a life event that triggers automatic activation of schemas;
- memories associated with schemas come into awareness;
- the memories activate possible ways of responding

48

- if the memories are related to trauma or other difficult events, four general types of schemas are activated:
  - pro-social
  - anti-social
  - self-destructive
  - dissociative

When a person relives trauma, the trigger is a fragment of the memory of the original trauma and serves as a reminder. Memories of trauma are usually fragmented. The fragments can be pieces of the trauma itself or the context in which the trauma takes place. The trigger can be a smell, a sight, a sound, a sensation, or a touch. In another words, one of the five senses. For example, a little girl who was sexually abused was locked for a time in a bathroom with a blinking purple light. When she sees the color purple, she remembers the sexual abuse and becomes anxious.

Memories have triggers, and so triggers can lead to activation of pleasant memories, such as when I see a doily my mother crocheted.

Whether triggers recall trauma or unhappy memories, our emotional reactions can be powerful. Allen (Allen & Poplack, n.d.) discussed the 90/20 principle. This stands for the idea that 90% of strong emotional reactions to unpleasant events are likely to be linked to unresolved past events and 10% to present circumstances. Some parents, for example, who have experienced childhood sexual abuse can be overwhelmed with emotion when they learn their own children have been sexually abused. Such an event is obviously difficult for any parent, but parents with unattended trauma may be so overwhelmed that they are unable to be sensitively responsive to their children. They may respond in preoccupied, dismissive, or disorganized ways.

Often the most emotionally powerful inner working models activate themselves first. In people who usually behave in pro-social ways, their initial schemas may be pro-social and so they act in pro-social ways. Often, however, people who behave in pro-social ways may sort through a variety of activated schemas. In these situations, schemas may engage in a kind of dialogue.

Dialoguing Schemas

Dialoguing schemas means that we appraise negative beliefs and positive beliefs that are composed of thoughts and images about the various courses of actions to take and their consequences. Fortunate people have IWMs that stop the processes of negative schemas with images and thoughts about negative consequences. Negative consequences that stop negative schemas include images of hurting others and the self through anti-social acts. Negative consequences also include images of hurting themselves and possibly others through self-destructive acts. Inappropriate acts are futile in that they don't really change situations. An example of inappropriate or ineffectual responses are playing the piano while the house burns down or doing nothing when someone harms a child. People realize that they do not want to bring about negative consequences and so they do not act on negative schemas.

Whichever sets of IWMs get the upper hand shapes individuals' responses to stressful events. Often the IWMs that have the upper hand shift over time, beginning perhaps with antisocial thoughts and images, activation of IWMs that show the negative consequences of the actions, then activation of IWMs that reject the negative consequences, and then the activation of pro-social schemas. What counts are the actions that arise from the activation and dialogue of schemas.

When negative actions takes place, such as anti-social or self-destructive acts, the schemas that have encoded anti-social or self-destruction beliefs and actions have dominated the IWMS that encoded pro-social beliefs and actions. Everyone has at least some prosocial IWMs, even very persons who have engaged in extreme acts of violence.

Sometimes the IWMs that activate themselves are so overwhelming that persons psychologically leave the scene. They may hum, pace, or even disassociate, which people can experience in many ways. One common way is to is to detach emotionally from whatever is going on in thoughts and images. Other ways are numbing, a sense of unreality, alterations of consciousness that can be a kind of forgetting where they are, even in a change of identity, and fugues, where people can travel to other places and not know how they got there. Disassociations, therefore, are on a continuum from mild, such as humming, to quite profound, such as the formation of new identities and fugue.

Strong Emotional Reactions Not Linked to Trauma

Some powerful emotional reactions are not linked to trauma but can be linked to how persons have learned to react to life events. In addition, some persons may have a kind of neurobiology that predisposes them to feel strongly and to be expressive emotionally in rather dramatic ways. In

50

these cases, their emotional reactions are normal to them. Only if their modes of emotional expressiveness cause problems for others and themselves might they consider teaching themselves new ways of self-expression.

Attachment and Trauma

Lieberman (2004) wrote that effective responses to children with relationship and mental health issues must have a dual trauma and attachment lens. Therefore, in assessing children and families where trauma has occurred, professionals assess for quality of attachment and the kinds of traumatic that may have occurred in the children and in the parents. They also inquire about how adults responded to children and how the children responded to adults. The responses of others in the children's lives are also important to assess.

The basic premise of Lieberman's work is the centrality of developing or restoring trust and intimacy between children and their parents, in other words in restoring security in attachment relationships. She works with both parents and children. With parents, she is supportive through listening and hearing their own experiences of trauma. She is sensitively responsive. She has noticed many times that when parents feel safe with her and understood, they then show capacities for being sensitively responsive to their own children. See details in Lieberman (2004), which is referenced at the end of this article.

Children develop capacities to cope with, adapt to, and overcome the effects of trauma within the safety of secure relationships. Secure attachments become safe havens where children express in their own ways what the trauma means to them and how trauma has affected them. They may express themselves with words, with toys and other objects, or through drawings and paintings. They could also show their role plays what the traumatic events mean to them. As they work their way through these meanings, adults are sensitively responsive and present to the children. Relaxation techniques such as yoga and meditation help children to regulate the stress of dealing directly with their trauma. Teaching children relaxation techniques before trauma therapy is becoming standard practice.

Thus, resilience is relational. Children learn to cope with, adapt to, and overcome the effects of trauma and adversities when they have safe havens where they process difficulty events. So do older children and adults. Resilience does not develop outside of relationships with others. As we grow older and develop increased capacities for coping, we may be able to process negative events well because we have internalized earlier experiences of successful coping. Responses that lead to resilience are encoded in our brain circuits. So, we are relating to people in our pasts even then, though symbolically. Still, many people in times of stress have a preference to process difficult issues with others.

Other Influences on IWMs

There are other influences on IWMs that may be unrelated to resilience but are related to anti-sociality. Examples of these influences are exposure to antisocial beliefs such as those that denigrate others and their actions. There are many beliefs that denigrate others, such those related to denying the dignity and worth of others and their rights to equal treatment and respect. Persons subject to denigration include GLBTQ individuals, undocumented immigrants, and persons with other than European heritages.

Resilience

Individuals show resilience when, in the face of stressful events, they act in pro-social ways. Persons cannot show resilience if they have not experienced stressful events. By definition, resilience represents capacities for coping with, adapting to, and overcoming risks, adversities, or stressful life events. Secure attachments and the pro-social IWMs that arise from secure attachments are key to coping with, adapting to, and overcoming negative life events. The latter is a definition of resilience, as stated earlier. Resilience processes become IWMs and are encoded in brain circuits. Thus, the foundation of resilience rests on secure attachments.

Neurological issues can interfere with the development of secure attachments. Children who have difficult temperaments or who have sensory issues related to touch may have compromised capacities for attachment. Further details on assessing for resilience when individuals have neurological issues are in the NEATS (Gilgun, 2011).

Prevention and Treatment

Successful treatment takes place within the safety of secure relationships where service providers become a secure base that support service users to discuss, reflect upon, and grapple with challenging issues. These challenging issues are often beliefs and expectations that interfere with quality of life. Trust builds when persons allow themselves to experience vulnerabilities in the presence of other persons who accept and validate their experiences. Feeling safe and trustful during times of vulnerability provide the foundation for recovery.

In treatment, professionals and clients seek to identify and build upon positive IWMs so as to develop them to the point where they overcome negative IWMs. In some instances, it is possible to change beliefs. This can be done in many ways. Confrontation does not work. People are likely to resist when others tell them their beliefs are harmful and they must change them. Of course, some people may change with confrontation but that means they also have many pro-social IWMs. Many people who do harmful things have rigid belief systems or inner working models that may be part of their identities and so difficult to change. Even people who tend to be self-destructive or dissociative may have rigid beliefs and expectations.

Changing beliefs that lead to actions that harm others and the self can be difficult and seemingly impossible, especially if individuals have a history of insecure attachments that give rise to mistrust if not hostility toward others and to rigid belief systems. Meditation and other relaxation techniques could be foundational to open persons with entrenched negative beliefs to examine them and experience them in new ways. Professionals can facilitate changing of beliefs, too. These include creating a safe space where individuals can express their beliefs any way they see fit, as long as these means are not harmful to self and others. Drawing people out by asking them to say more about their beliefs may over time lead them to realize that other beliefs may serve them and others in more fair and caring ways.

Parent-Child Psychotherapy and Infant Mental Health programs have research that demonstrates their effectiveness in work with families and children where trauma has occurred (Lieberman, 2004). Other programs and treatment approaches that have proven effectiveness are EMDR, dialectic behavior therapy, and Circle of Security. The first two were developed for work with adults, although there are versions now for younger people.

The Circle of Security program is psychoeducational in nature. Psychoeducation involves the provision of information to participants in educational programs, such as information about trauma, attachment, and recovery. Psychoeducation programs also engage in a series of exercises that encourage participants to reflect upon their present beliefs and expectations and support participants in new behaviors and expectations.

Program participants also have many opportunities to express their responses to the educational material and to the new behaviors they practice. Effective programs are safe havens.

The key issue is for professionals to become safe havens and secure bases where individuals can explore, examine, grapple with, and assess their life experiences and beliefs. In other words, for service users to develop resilience where they have vulnerabilities, they must develop relationships of trust with service providers.

Professionals recognize the many influences on human functioning and thus work with clients on how to deal with the many stressors that may arise in their interactions with persons and situations in the many settings in which they live their lives. Doing so pays attention to the social ecologies of the persons we work with. Social ecologies are the various environments in which individuals live their lives, such as family, school, neighborhood, religious organizations, and work.

In family and couples therapy, the goal is to develop relationships of trust with spouses and children. In group therapy and psychoeducation, relationships with group members and program participants are also important for the development of resilience. These relationships of trust are in addition to trust for service providers. Thus in these modes of treatment, individuals have several relationships that help them with their vulnerabilities to deal with resilience.

Concluding Thoughts

Persons develop resilience through relationships with others, beginning with secure relationships in infancy and then continuing throughout the life course. When we have secure relationships, we are much more likely to deal with negative life events through seeking comfort and help from people we trust. Resilience is a positive response to adversities that develops when others are sensitively responsive and dependable.

IWMs are composed of beliefs that guide actions. When persons have histories of secure attachments and have experienced trauma, they may be open to change. People with secure attachments tend to have trust, empathy, and openness to new ideas.

Persons with histories of insecure attachments may find trust difficult. They have learned from experience that when they have been stressed or have experienced traumas, others have not been there for them and helped them to develop resilience.

They may be resistant to new ideas and may have little empathy for themselves and for others. In these cases, professionals will find themselves more challenged than in working with persons with histories of secure attachments. The goal is to encourage people to examine their IWMs. This may involve first teaching people relaxation techniques and meditation in order to help them to learn to cope with the powerful emotions that arise when traumas are triggered in treatment. Relaxation and meditation may also help people access their beliefs and expectations and thus be helpful when the time comes to talk about them.

Trauma work for professionals also involves a lot of listening and empathy. Eventually even clients who mistrust and have rigid beliefs may grow in capacities to trust and may begin to question their own beliefs. Eventually, they may develop more positive IWMs and changes in their beliefs. They may develop undeveloped pro-social inner working models and even develop new ones. These pro-social IWMs lead to increases pro-social behaviors and decreases in anti-social, self-destructive, and dissociative behaviors.

Because human beings are relational, treatment and interventions programs take into account social ecologies. Thus, in individual work, much of the effort is on understanding and re-interpreting family relationships and relationships with others. Couple and family therapy offer opportunities for clients to develop new ways of understanding and relating to the people with whom they have close relationships. Case management with survivors of trauma often involves coaching clients to deal with difficult situations at clients' social ecologies and may also include advocacy on behalf of clients.

Finally, professionals who work in the areas of trauma, attachment, and recovery put themselves at risk to experience secondary trauma, sometimes called vicarious trauma. Being exposed to the trauma stories of others can be traumatizing. Therefore, professionals would do well to engage in reflective practice so as to monitor their own emotional states and mental health. They would do well to eat well, sleep well, engage in recreation, and seek the company of affirming people. They may at times require the special support that supervision and consultation can provide. Individual and group therapy, meditation, and various relaxation techniques may help practitioners maintain balance in their lives and thus to continue to be effective in their work and in their personal lives.

In summary, resilience is relational and therefore develops from relationships with others. Professionals are helpful to persons who have experienced trauma when they are safe havens. Allen told a story about the importance of professionals as safe havens. He said to a group of students, "The mind can be a scary place." A student responded, "Yes, and you wouldn't want to go in there alone." Professionals are companions for people who are dealing with difficult life events. Other people also are safe havens for us in times of stress and trauma.

References

Gilgun, Jane F. (2011).*The NEATS: A Child & Family Assessment*. Amazon.

Hoffman, K., Marvin, R., Cooper, G. & Powell, B. (2006). Changing toddlers' and preschoolers' attachment classifications: The Circle of Security Intervention. *Journal of Consulting and Clinical Psychology, 74,* 1017-1026.

Lieberman, Alicia F. (2004). Traumatic stress and quality of attachment: Reality and internalization in disorders of infant mental health. *Infant Mental Health Journal, 25(4),* 336-351.

Rutter, Michael (2012). Resilience as a dynamic concepts. *Development and Psychopathology, 24,* 335-344.

8

The Meanings of Violence to Perpetrators: Intimations of What Was Ahead

In this chapter, I reflect upon the early days of my research on violence. I continually questioned myself about why I was doing it. The research traumatized me. Yet, I persisted. I was determined to understand what violence means to perpetrators. I gradually began to understand violence as I understood violence in my own heart. This chapter is an account of the transformations I experienced as I did my research. The chapter is an excerpt from Gilgun, Jane F. (2008). Lived experience, reflexivity, and research on perpetrators of interpersonal violence. Qualitative Social Work, *7(2), 181-197.*

I did not know it at the time, but my first visit to a maximum security prison was a preview of how the research would affect me personally. The following description of this first visit are from fieldnotes I wrote while I did the research.

> The steel doors clanged shut behind me. The sound shivered up my spine and bounced against the steel-reinforced concrete walls of the stairwell. Head lowered, I walked down the steps and stopped in front of the door at the bottom of the stairwell. My escort said his name into a small square grate next to the door. Someone I could not see hit a switch. The door rumbled open. I walked through. The door rumbled back into its frame and clanged shut behind me.

> So it went. Through five sliding, rumbling, clanging steel doors, down five steel-reinforced concrete stairways until I arrived at the treatment unit of the maximum security prison, Minnesota Correctional Facility-Oak Park Heights. Five thick steel doors stood between me and the outside. I felt as if I had descended into hell.

I had. For the years that followed, I listened to the stories prisoners told me. Through their eyes, I witnessed murders, attempted murders, child molestations, rapes, woman battering, and physical assaults. Often these men committed other crimes, such as robberies, burglaries, and criminal vehicular homicide, all of which added to my understanding. Their focus on what they wanted and their disregard for survivors and victims at the time they committed violent acts both astonished and terrified me. The recklessness and self endangerment of some of their behaviors provided additional dimensions to my understanding of what violence meant to them.

Early on, the impact of the stories led me to question why I was doing the research. One of the first times I questioned myself was after an interview with a man who had molested his own children and children of friends and employers. The man told a detailed story of the murder of a runaway girl and her burial in a cornfield. In fieldnotes, I wrote about what I had been thinking as he talked.

> I was wondering what I was doing there listening to someone talk about the murder of a 14 year-old runaway. The answer came later-- because you want to stop this horror, but it is so horrible to listen to it.

At first, the effects were almost more than I could bear. For instance, one sunny day after a particularly difficult interview, I had lunch with a friend at an outdoor café. She asked me about the interview. As I shared the vivid descriptions the informant had given of the strangulation murders of his fiancée, an unrelated woman, and his two toddler children (Gilgun, 1999a), I experienced intense anxiety. All of a sudden, I felt I was high in the sky, as if tethered to a helium-filled balloon. I looked down at the two of us sitting at the small round table, engaged in conversation.

Mental health professionals call this an out-of-body experience, linked to disassociation, which is a way of distancing ourselves from stressful and perhaps traumatic experiences. In my case, this response was secondary traumatization or vicarious traumatization that can happen when persons are exposed to the traumas that others have suffered (Campbell, 2002; Cunningham, 2003). Apparently, I had entered vicariously into the experiences of the women and children whose victimization a perpetrator had described in detail.

> That night I dreamed I was naked in a public place. My body was more trim and shapely than I thought it was in actuality. This was no consolation. Apparently, I had felt overly exposed when I talked to my friend. In fieldnotes, I wrote that she had done

nothing to trigger anxiety and, apparently, shame. She was a model of interest and compassion.

Connected Knowing

Over time, there were changes in how the research affected me and how I understood violence. After about five years of interviewing perpetrators, I put together two different aspects of violence that had formerly been separate in my mind -- as entertainment in various media and as brutal and horrible in real time with real people in real situations. I wrote

What am I doing there listening to such stuff? I am there because I want to understand

> it so I can stop it. The horror is real. For the first time, I have an in-the-bones understanding of what violence is. It is not funny. It's not stylized. People don't pop back to life, like cartoon characters after they've been run over by a steamroller. They stay dead. They stay maimed. They carry their psychological pain forever, and it influences how they think, feel, and act. This horror must stop, and I want a part in stopping it.

This in-the-bones knowing is a synonym for *connected knowing* and *vicarious experience*. I was now into connected knowing, a knowledge that I still think of as walking into the jaws of hell.

To get to connected knowing, I first endured raw experience that took time to transform into knowledge. Knowledge requires reflections on experience recollected in tranquility, as Wordsworth said of the relationship between emotions and poetry. My sense of being tethered to a helium-filled balloon and my nightmare of being unclothed in a public place were raw experiences, unmediated by thought and far from tranquil.

Raw reactions also included re-living what appeared to be every slight and trauma I had experienced over my lifetime. I wanted to tell others about these responses, but I felt too vulnerable to expose my distress to family and friends. I was unsure that they could help me anyway, and I did not want to risk traumatizing them. I chose instead to work with a therapist on a weekly basis for several years. Within the safety of a therapeutic relationship, I was able to grapple with and let go of many troubling memories and emotions.

Getting beyond my own hurts and trauma appeared to have cleared the way for me to develop a capacity to ask for more detail in the telling of the stories, details that informants appeared glad to provide. The following passage illustrates getting beyond my own hurts and enlarged capacities to face up to what violence is to perpetrators and survivors. I wrote these notes after an interview with a man who was in prison for molesting children.

> I was astonished more than anything to get this detail. I never had the courage before to ask him about the detail. I'm sure he would have told me. It's not courage. It's stomach. I have had to work very hard on myself -- to get to the point where I could bear these details. My life hurts and losses sound trivial compared to what happened to these girls, but I experienced my own childhood pain as so awful that I had to be very careful in uncovering it, transforming it, so that I could bear to hear about the oppression of others. I have often wondered why I was willing to spend the time I have spent to work through the pain I have worked through in order to listen to such stories.

Eventually, my own hurts were in the background. Foremost was my concern for what victims and survivors had endured. I wrote

> I cried a lot the day after I talked to him -- on Saturday, which was yesterday. I was glad to cry, and the crying no longer is about me and my losses. The crying was for that young woman and her family and the cruelty and irony and unfeelingness of Mack [not his real name], for the horror of waking up and seeing someone in your room, someone you'd recognize, and to have your life taken by his hands around your throat.

Mack and the young woman he murdered were first-year students at a land-grant university. Mack had noticed her the day they both had arrived on campus. She and he lived on different floors in the same dorm. The only time he spoke to her was a few days before he raped and murdered her. They were getting food in the cafeteria. He said

I was reaching for some butter. She reached at the same time. She laughed and said 'Excuse me.' I also said, 'Excuse me.' I was half asleep. I just woke up from a nap. She said, 'Go ahead.' I said, 'No, go ahead.' She laughed and picked up some butter. I picked my butter up and went and sat down and ate.

She did not know that she had looked into the eyes of the young man who would murder her.

My Rage

Another aspect of my response to Mack's story was rage. The rage evoked in me an imagined act of violence. This is what I wrote in response to Mack's account of the murder.

> As he talked, an image of a bullet hole between his eyes came unbidden into my mind. I thought I had shot him though I had not moved as he told his story. I was sick at heart. Later, I was enraged over what he had done. Anna [not her real name] was nothing to him, an object maybe, but not a human being, not a young woman at the brink of her adult life, with a future to look forward to. He couldn't even pronounce *strangle* right, adding to the absurdity and horror. I could not conjure up any milk of human kindness toward him. What could have happened to him to make him think that this is what he could do to Anna? Or any other woman?

He described the murder as accidental. He explained, "I did not want to strangulate her. I only wanted to render her unconscious so I could rape her." The so-called accidental nature of the murder was horrible enough, but his mispronunciation of the word *strangle* was especially irritating, something trivial from many points of view, but the mispronunciation might have been my tipping point to where, without a conscious act of will, something inside of me wanted him dead.

In my mind, I had shot him. I had no images in my mind of picking up a gun and shooting, but I knew I had done it in my imagination. I doubt this is what Robert Park meant when he advised students to participate vicariously in the lives of informants -- or maybe this is what he did mean. I remember feeling surprised at the image and then detached. I may have experienced a smudge of satisfaction that he was dead, that he deserved it, and that a bullet between his eyes had stopped his earnest narration of horror. These are themes that I have seen repeatedly in the narratives of the perpetrators I have interviewed (Gilgun, 1998).

Connected Knowing

This experience is far from what I had expected when I set out to understand violence from perpetrators' points of view. I did not know that I would discover that I am capable of murder, at least in my imagination,

61

and that I would take satisfaction in murder. My violent reactions to Mack's story did not end with the interview. I wrote in fieldnotes

> After the interview, the tension built all day. By nightfall, I was screaming at other drivers for slowing down to make a turn or for stopping at an amber traffic light.

The irony of this description of my own violence processes is that I was unaware of them until I was immersed in the research. For instance, I sometimes cursed and yelled at drivers who cut me off on highways and imagined slamming into them. I would laugh at myself for being so ridiculous but there was a satisfaction, a pleasure in imagining doing so. Like clockwork, however, images of bloodied bodies and crushed cars stopped my enjoyment. I never reflected on these violent outbursts and so they remained outside of my awareness.

This subconscious fantasy, however, was key to my understanding the satisfaction that violence typically brings to perpetrators in real time with real persons in real situations. The first instance of the connections I made between an account of violence and my own experience involved several elements: an informant who sold heroin, a dog, a woman who wanted heroin but had no money, a video camera, and a four or five other men who were present to view the performance the informant orchestrated. This is what the informant said

> She said, 'I'll do anything' As soon as I heard that then, there it is. It was like I was God and the white leader. It was like all these people were laughing and making comments. It was like I made this happen. It wasn't just her and the dog itself. It was like the other people, too. There were at least four or five other guys.

As he spoke, I remember thinking that this is not my idea of God. I also remembered other conversations we had had about how much he enjoyed the power he had over others, with this episode an example. Soon afterward, maybe as I was driving home, a driver cut me off. I went into my usual routine of yelling and cursing, laughing, imaging slamming into the other car, the blood and gore, and the end of the fantasy.

I flashed on this man's statement of feeling like God, of his obvious pleasure in recalling the memory, and of my horrified reactions. Then I saw that my own violent fantasies gave me pleasure, made me laugh. I got it. I connected to the joy that many perpetrators experience in their violent acts. For the first time, I understood the joy of violence. The obvious difference between me and them was that they acted out violence while I simply enjoyed myself in fantasy. This is a crucial difference, but the similarities are now obvious to me.

Violence as Self-Puffery

There was some self-puffery in my over-the-top reactions to the reckless driving of others. I saw plenty of self-puffery in the stories perpetrators told. These stories gave me insight into my own bravado. Cory [not his real name] provided one of many lessons on the pleasures of self-puffery. He said

> When somebody's done something or what not, I'll say to myself, I'll use my exact words. 'You fucking dickhead, you have no idea of who you're even saying that to. I'll rip your skull off.' That sense of power is inside of me. It's always there, that sense of power, how powerful you are. Okay? I go, 'Listen to you.' That will be my exact words. 'If you only knew. If you only knew.'

Cory backed up his words with actions. He habitually got into bar fights and was in prison for almost beating his wife to death while his toddler daughter screamed and cried. His talk about how powerful he is gave me insight into what I gain when I threaten other drivers. Like a gorilla who beats her chest, my displays on the highway were fun, bluff. They lifted my mood. I felt fear and anger when someone else's recklessness threatened my physical and emotional safety. Unlike Cory, I did not actually mean what I said and fantasized about.

Connecting to the Emotions
but Not the Deeds

My connected knowing of what violence might mean to perpetrators did not always involve tapping into the violence within me. For example, I cannot connect to the chills and thrills that Don [not his real name] expressed in regard to rape, but I do know the happiness of anticipating other events, such as a trip abroad or a gourmet meal. Don, convicted of seven rapes, was a high school athlete and a graduate of an elite private college (Gilgun & McLeod, 1999). This is what he told me about looking for women to rape:

> Well, nothing ever gave me the intense kind of feeling. Especially like when I was driving around, and I would be thinking about it, maybe following somebody, I had like a physical reaction. I would

be shaking, physically shaking, like teeth would chatter. I couldn't stop. It wouldn't stop. I never had that kind of physical reaction to anything else. I would also get like butterflies. I can relate that to sports events, before a big game or something, that feeling but not the physical.

Don meant that he did not have an erection before high school football games but did when he was driving around looking for a woman to rape. His description is convincing. I understand from my own experience how intense his anticipation might have been, although chills and thrills in anticipating rape is far outside of my frame of reference.

Also outside of my frame of reference was how he viewed the women he victimized. In fact, I was incredulous when he told me, "Rape is not personal. If one of my victims walked in the room right now, I wouldn't recognize her." For me rape is a horrifyingly personal assault. The rapes Don described brought to mind images of a hairy, hard body slamming into mine, a frenzied, brutish grab at my clothes and neck, a fist slamming into my face, and the horror of the penetration. Then, being left like rubbish. Rape is not *personal*? Fear of rape terrorizes women, and few get into their cars, especially after dark, before taking a look into the back seat to see if anyone is hiding there.

So, I did not connect with Don's experience of rape. Thrills do not well up in me as I think about raping someone. In fact, until I wrote that sentence I have never before thought about what it would mean to me to rape someone. Some of the stories perpetrators tell are outside of my frame of reference. I can enter only so far into their experiences. It appears that I can understand some of the emotions they feel but not the situations in which they feel them.

Yet, I know what impersonal encounters are. On the basis of that personal knowledge, I believe him when he said that rape is not personal. I had to develop a capacity to see that there is more than one view of rape. I experienced cognitive dissonance when he said rape is not personal but I believed him immediately. His affect was convincing.

Paradoxically, Don's shocking statement about the impersonal nature of rape is liberating. It means that rape survivors do not have responsibility for rape. Rape is about what perpetrators want. Rape has nothing to do with potential or actual victims. Survivors and victims are persons who were in the presence of rapists who set up the situation so that no else was around to interfere.

Layers of Meaning

As I accepted the violence in my own heart and realized there are some experiences that are outside of my personal frame of reference, I gradually was able to connect to additional meanings that violence has for perpetrators. For instance, in the first of many interviews with Alan (not his real name), I inquired about his marital status, he said, "You could say I'm a widower" with a tone of irony (Gilgun, 1999a). What he said and how he said it confused me. I asked him how his wife had died. These are my reflections.

> ...it did not occur to me that his wife had been murdered. I was genuinely confused about how she had died until he told me about the lime pit. [Her skeleton was found in a lime pit. The man who found her knew it was a human skeleton because of the red polish on her fingernails.] It was disturbing to me to hear him talk about this because there was an erotic component from him, a heavy erotic component, a sense of having gotten away with something and enjoying that, and a sense of being in a funeral home -- a sort of heavy, ominous sense of finality. I wonder if I was experiencing some of his grief.

This, I think, is an example of connected knowing. Like the incident with the bullet hole where I apparently acted out a murder, my sense of connection to his emotions happened all by itself, without a conscious act of will on my part. I identified his emotions through an intuitive connection. I, too, have experienced satisfaction, veiled amusement, eroticism, and grief, not, however, in regard to a murder that I actually did commit. (The police investigated Alan for the murder but did not have enough evidence to charge him. Alan's affect told me that he had killed her.) Alan also did not express remorse, either in words or through non-verbal means. In my imagined shooting of Mack, at that moment, I too had no remorse.

My point is that I understand some of the aspects of violence through connected knowing, but that there are dimensions of perpetrators' accounts that are outside of my frame of reference and outside of my capacities to connect. Even though I may fantasize about violent acts, this is far from actually committing them. Insofar as I immerse myself in the informants worlds and open myself up to their accounts, however, I appear to be developing an in-depth understanding of the meanings of violence to perpetrators.

Discussion

As I reflect on my lived experiences as a feminist woman conducting life history research with men who had perpetrated interpersonal violence, I see how much of what I now know stems from connected knowing. When I designed the study on which this article is based, I applied the principles that had served me well in conducting research on girl survivors of child sexual abuse. This prior research also gave me the hope that audiences would be as receptive to learning about interpersonal violence from perpetrators as they were about learning about child sexual abuse from girl survivors.

In retrospect, after more than 20 years of research on perpetrators, I see how naïve I was. My gain in understanding exacted a price. I questioned myself many times. To get to what might be connected knowing, I experienced horror, fear, and pity at what I had vicariously witnessed, I relived and worked through past hurts, and I identified with victims and survivors. These processes appeared to have enabled me to connect in new and deeper ways with what victims and survivors might have gone through. In short, my responses shifted from personal fears and stress to concern for what victims and survivors might have endured.

Working though my own reactions appeared also to have led to capacities to catch the layers of meanings that violent acts might have for perpetrators. Finally, this research also brought to awareness the satisfactions I derive from thinking violent thoughts.

I am quite sure that I will never not react to violence. For instance, in writing this article, I found myself occasionally over-reacting to events that I otherwise would have approached with more internal peace. Although I have increased capacities for dealing with violence, immersion into the transcripts of the interviews led to a sense of once more of feeling as if I were being ground up. My responses are not as intense as they once were. They are fleeting in comparison to earlier stressful reactions.

I do not enjoy my violent fantasies as much as I used to. They pop up much less often, though I could be fooling myself. I am sometimes tempted to make angry gestures at other drivers who behave rudely or dangerously on motorways, but images of some of the men I have interviewed flash into mind. I think I had better not. Who knows how they will react? Furthermore, I do not want to be like persons who perpetrate violence. I do not want to commit violent acts even vicariously. My anticipation of the fun of self-puffery is cut short by such thoughts.

I stuck with this research out of concern for victims and survivors. I was convinced that the in-depth knowledge of perpetrators would contribute to prevention. I assumed that the identification and understanding of a social problem compose the first steps toward major change efforts. Had I not believed this, I would have stopped doing the research as soon as the going got tough.

Today, I am less convinced that such is the case. Violence is endemic world-wide. Countless persons use violent means of redressing perceived wrongs, motivated typically by attitudes such as, You don't know who you're dealing with, I'm the man, and You can't mess with me. What violence means to perpetrators of interpersonal violence also appears to have similar meanings to persons who commit violence in the name of social justice and to bring about political and social change.

I am less convinced for another reason. The selling of violence as fun and as entertainment is far too embedded in American culture to change. The profit motive that subsidizes and glamorizes violence could be the case world-wide. It is as if there is a split consciousness between violence as fun, violence as a solution, and violence as tragedy.

It has taken me two decades to arrive at my present understandings of the violence of others and the violence in myself. I have no idea how many other people are willing to subject themselves to what I have subjected myself to in order to gain the connected knowing I think I now have. Maybe connected knowing is not necessary to be concerned enough about violence to do something about it, even in little ways in our daily lives.

It seems to me, though, that any concerted effort toward violence prevention would have to encompass the multiple meanings of violence and not just the tragic aspect of it. The effects on victims and survivors and the effects on quality of life in families, neighborhoods, and worldwide compose just one aspect of violence.

Despite my less than optimistic view of what lies ahead for violence prevention, I believe that those who want to do something about it should carry on. There is much to be said about what violence means to perpetrators and much to be done to prevent violence and to be responsive to those who survive violence. The more we know about what violence means to perpetrators, the more effective we will be to change the conditions that lead people to be violent in the first place.

Finally, with knowledge of what violence means to perpetrators, survivors will be more likely to know in their bones that they did nothing to deserve to be victimized. Survivors will have in-the-bones knowledge that perpetrators alone are responsible for their acts of violence.

References

Belenky, Mary Field, Blythe McVicker Clinchy, Nancy Rule Goldberger, & Jill Mattuck Trule (1986). *Women's ways of knowing: The development of self, voice, and mind.* New York: Basic.

Benner, Patricia (Ed.) (1994). *Interpretive phenomenology.* Thousand Oaks, CA: Sage.

Campbell, Rebecca (2002). *Emotionally involved: The impact of researching rape.* New York: Routledge.

Cunningham, Maddy (2003). Impact of trauma work on social work clinicians: Empirical findings. *Social Work, 48(4),* 451-459.

Gilgun, Jane F. (1998, November). A comprehensive theory of family violence. Paper presented at Preconference Workshop on Theory Construction & Research Methodology, National Council on Family Relations, Milwaukee, WI. www.mincava.umn.edu/gilgun/brainstrm.htm.

Gilgun, Jane F., & Laura McLeod (1999). Gendering violence. *Studies in Symbolic Interactionism, 22,* 167-193.

9

The Tough-Talkin' Tee Shirt
as Public Pedagogy

A tee-shirt with a six-cylinder handgun pointing directly out. The words "We don't dial 911: Texas." This tee-shirt hung in the window of a San Antonio, Texas, USA, store. I thought of 17 year-old Trayvon Martin shot dead two years ago in Florida by a man who apparently believed what was on the tee-shirt. Many other people do, too. In fact, the idea is law in some states. Stand your ground laws say it's ok to shoot someone if you think you are in danger. No need to call 911. That is the defense the man who shot Trayvon used. The jury agreed, and he was declared not guilty.

The message on the tee-shirt is tough talk, for some the mark of a real man and self-evident in its simplicity. For others, the message is appalling and gives permission to shoot first and ask questions later. For scholars, the message on the tee-shirt is an example of how people learn what they are supposed to believe and how they are supposed to act. They call this kind of learning *public pedagogy*.

We tend to think we learn in schools and in families, but public spaces like store windows, neighborhood interactions, and electronic media are sources of teaching and learning, too. We are bombarded with messages that shape what we think and tell us how we are supposed to behave.

The ideas behind public pedagogy challenges violent prevention efforts. People like me who want to prevent violence and promote optimal living conditions have quite a job. The countless pro-violence messages that we receive daily teach us how to behave. The messages are forthright and direct. What a rush. I'm a man. I shoot. I don't dial 911. What in the world counteracts that?

After many years, I believe we can make an effort one person at a time. Parents can use tee-shirts and other conveyers of anti-social messages as teachable moments where they discuss the advantages of calling 911 and the disadvantages of shooting someone. Many parents, however, teach their children that not calling 911 and shooting someone are wise words.

Taking a step back, violence prevention advocates can promote polices and programs that support parents to raise children who see violence as counterproductive. Parents who do this are sensitively responsive to their children from birth and show by actions and words prosocial ways of getting what you want and accepting that you can't always get what you want. Children raised this way not only become pro-social and see the benefits of prosociality, but they also see pro-violence messages as foolish, as reckless, as acting without thinking through consequences.

People who state they are devout Christians or members of other religious faiths may realize that the greatest commandment is love and that every religion says that the divine principle is in every one of us. Such thoughts make violence impossible—until we disconnect from them. Then the violence we internalized can become actual

Other necessary components of effective violence prevention are policy makes. It would take a miracle for policy makers to suddenly turn into creative thinkers who anticipate the consequences of their actions. Imagine how everything would change if they brought values of caring and social justice into their thinking. Then their polices might promote healthy families and communities that have the recreational, educational, and economic resources that their own neighborhoods have. Changes in policies and practice are required for the prevention of violence.

I don't know how to push back against the public pedagogy of pro-violence values and beliefs except through education and advocacy. Compared to the forces that support violence, advocates of non-violence are puny. Far too many people benefit, or think they do, from ideologies of violence

While writing this I'm watching a video. The scene that just played was of four men fighting with six others. The four were the good guys. The hero said, "We don't kill. We only disable." So they proceeded to hit the bad guys with fists and big wooden rakes. For good measure they kicked one of the guys in the groin. That was supposed to be funny. The camera pulled back for a long shot with four men laid out unconscious and the good guys standing over them triumphant. The entire scene has bouncy music intended to convey fun and humor.

I hope that pro-social forces do public pedagogy as skillfully as those who do anti-social public pedagogy. As I think about this, I know many people who promote pro-sociality. May they push back effectively. It's going to take a lot.

Reference

Giroux, Henry A. (2004). Cultural studies, public pedagogy, and the responsibility of intellectuals. *Communication and Critical/Cultural Studies, 1(1)*, 59-79.

10

The Death of George the Duck
Teaches me a Lesson

I will no longer be silent about the horrors of violence.

Gorge the duck was murdered in July 2013 at her home in River Walk, San Antonio, Texas, USA. Her last minutes were caught on a web cam. Late at night, two men in white t-shirts grabbed George, who was sleeping next to a lamp post. They laughed and shouted as they held her by the neck, kicked her, wrung her neck, and then sauntered down the walk as she dangled dead from their hands. They threw her into the San Antonio River, laughing all the way.

For years, George was an attraction for tourists and San Antonians alike. She'd walk up to people as if knew them and often posed with them for photos and videos. She also has babies. Her husband was a mallard, and so the babies don't look like George, but they carry her genes and hopefully her spirit.

A Tipping Point

I just learned the story of George the duck and immediately decided that my decades-long reluctance is over. Never again, not ever, will hold back on telling stories of what violence means to perpetrators and what it's like to be the target of violence. Never again will I worry that if I sensationalize violence when I tell the stories I have heard. The death of George, a duck, has struck me deeply as cruel and horrific. That chord is far too familiar.

The laughing glee of the murderers reminds me of the glee that I heard as people they told me stories of the violence they committed—on people and sometimes on animals, such as sodomizing a chicken. One man told me that he got the best orgasms when he had penetrated a chicken and then slammed her head in a door. The spasm of the chicken was exquisite. Ecstasy.

Get it? I'm done pussy footing and moly coddling. If readers don't want to know what violence is like, I encourage them not to read this article. Stop right here. Stop when you get to the chicken part. Stop when you get to "George the duck was murdered." You may have good reasons why you don't want to read such stuff. Take care of yourself. Do what you've got to do. To be honest, another reason I haven't published most of what I've already written because the stories sometimes traumatize me. Well, I have to find the resources to push back against violence by telling other people what violence is.

It's time for me and the rest of us who can bear it to dig in and take a good hard look at violence. Let's join my Sicilian relatives who say "Basta" when they've had enough. I've had enough. Basta. The death of George the duck was my tipping point. I've had enough of violence.

Here goes.

The following is one of the hundreds of stories I've written and never published. This story will show you what violence is for one human being. So will the other stories I have to tell. Stay tuned. I'm going to publish them. Maybe you will reach your tipping point and do something about violence. Thank you, George. You have many legacies.

The Story of a Serial Rapist
Who Experienced
the Abuse of Children as Love

This is what a man in prison told me about his sexual abuse of children and his rapes of women.

I would actually go through mental battles before I raped. It would be like, it was like I was two different people. I'd be talking. Sometimes I'd even talk verbally: "You can't do this." The one that was saying, "You can't do this," was real gentle, docile type individual. The one that was the, "Yeah, I can do this," was a real belligerent, evil, what I consider evil type individual.

Eventually it would come down to the dominant one would just tell the docile one, "Fuck you. Shut the fuck up. We're going to do this," and that's the way it would come out. That's the way it would be and (finger snap) the other one would just disappear.

73

All the time that the rapes were going on, it would be like this one would be standing up there watching and would be in pain about it. The dominant one would feel powerful. Just seemed like every time I raped that individual got more and more and more and more powerful. The other one got weaker and weaker because it's like I was losing part of me.

I wasn't beating them because I would snatch them up by the neck and apply just enough pressure to get them to consent. They knew they were going to die. They would give in. I'd just tell them, "You're going do every damn thing I tell you to do. You have no choice." That's the way it was. I didn't beat anybody up. I didn't hit women. My ma told me, "You don't hit women," and I never hit women.

I was the greatest around kids. You know what I'm saying (chuckle)? That's the part that's so messed up. I can play with kids. They'll all have fun and they'll all want to be there with me, have a good time.

With kids, it's weird. It was like warm, comfortable, gentle. It was like making love. I think it's the other type individual if it's with children, the one that was docile and stuff. Kids—it's where he belonged. That's where he fit in. There wasn't anybody threatening him. When it was more powerful, put pressure on him. I don't know how to explain it. (big sigh)

It was like, all right, like you could be a threat, okay, if you were there, okay, because you're an adult. You could threaten this other type of individual, the small, docile one. When he's with kids, okay, he could have power over kids because they couldn't hurt him in any way. So he had his power there because you don't hit women. I don't know why I wanted to be sexual with kids.

The love, the love that I experienced, the gentleness that I ever experienced, the caring that I ever experienced in my life came from Kyle Wallace. The price for all that was having sex with him. Okay? He was gentle with me. He was kind to me. Okay? He didn't hit me. He didn't threaten me. That was the same type of stuff that I did with kids. I enjoyed sex with Kyle.

I went through a thing about being a homosexual about that. That was really weird. I was nine, ten, eleven, twelve until I got into the state training school. Four or five years I was sexual with Kyle. My father was beating me with a rubber hose. It's just a flip flop. Sex started with Kyle and I. He used to take a couple of us kids swimming. Then he just started taking me by myself.

When I was in the state training school, that was incorrigibility but that was for like child molesting. I was messing with kids that were like my own age.

74

They really didn't call it child molesting because it was all the same age. This was going on like when I was ten, eleven, twelve years old. I was also being molested at that time, too, by Kyle, who owned the farm next door. He molested other boys, too. He never got caught.

My mother's boyfriend used to come home drunk and beat my ma. I used to jump on him and hide the kids first and then jump on him until he would get off her and start beating on me. Then she'd get away, and then I'd get away. That was the normal pattern when he came home. I shot at him with a shotgun, just beebees, hit him in the back. He was on the porch, and I shot from the living room. Most of the beebeees hit the porch. Some of them went into him.

They took me to a state home. I wanted to kill that man. I was eight. I went to a juvenile orphanage home. It was a farm. I was the youngest person there, too. That's where I learned to love animals.

I was also raped when I was six. Three teenagers that I didn't know. They made me suck them off, and they did me in the butt. Just about anything that they wanted to do. They told me they'd kill me if I told. I was with a friend. I told him to run away. He did. I never saw him again. He lived right across the street from me. I stopped wanting to live a long time. I stopped wanting to live when I got raped. Yet I wouldn't tell anybody. They said they'd kill me if I told. That kept me from telling so I must have wanted to live.

I think I was mixed up because I thoughts when I was a kid to shoot myself and stuff. I knew how to handle guns. My father taught me how to handle guns real well. I was a real good shot. I knew what it would take to kill somebody and what it would take to kill myself. I think I was in the process of making that decision. I never let anybody know anything about me. Why should I? I figured I wasn't going to be around long enough anyway.

I know I had a lot of hatred just towards everybody, mainly men. I always felt like I had no power over men. I think it had a lot to do with why I rape women because I could get power over them but I couldn't get it over a man.

Then I almost killed myself on drugs when I was about seventeen. I went to the hospital and the doctor that I was seeing told me, he says, "You want some help? We got some people who will come up here and talk to you." They took some tests on me, and these two guys come in, little snooty looking guys. One of them told me I was paranoid schizophrenic and should be locked up for the rest of my life (laugh). So I kind of told him to kiss my

75

feet. Then my doctor that was treating me for malnutrition and other stuff that I was into asked me if I really wanted to get some help. I said, "Yeah, I do,"

If you let people get close all that results in that is that you get hurt. You either get hurt because they turn around and walk away. I still have that belief. That anybody you get close to is going to leave. Period. So I'm already prepared for that. Kind of a real funky way to go into a relationship with anybody but that's the way it is, you know.

The other part of it is that if it's men they're going to want sex from you if they get close. So you don't let them close. That way you don't have to give them sex. Right? To this day at 42 years old if I get into a room with a man I'm very nervous. I don't allow anybody to know it, but I'm very nervous because I think that's what's coming.

I think the day that I stop feeling like that will be the day that I know I have enough power and control not to hurt people.

Now there's some bestiality into this too, for about three years in my early twenties. It was bizarre. I was doing a lot of drugs. A horse and cow. That's having sex with animals. This is going to be real gross, but this is the way it was. It seemed like sex to me was just a place to dump your nut.

I can't think of a better way to put it. That's just the way it was in my head, even including sex that I had with women. I was living with a girl name Sam. I used to have sex with her two, three times a day. It was just like a better place to masturbate. I know its sounds weird but that's the way it was. I've never been satisfied sexually. It was more like my dick was a weapon, was a gun. This is how I brutalize. Instead of hitting women this is what I did to them because you can't hit women.

I would make women give me oral sex, anal sex, vaginal sex. Whatever I wanted, that's what I did. Whatever I wanted them to do, I made sure they did. Powerful. Nobody could hurt me.

You get the release and the feel good. I think that's why there was so much sex with my victims. It was just because I'd give a nut and then two minutes later I'm hard, and I want to go do it again. My last victim, I had her for eleven hours in a hotel room having sex with her. You know, that's (sigh) not normal behavior when you gun several nuts.

When I'm in a relationship, it's kind of the way I show I love--having sex with them. I've tried to explain it to people and they have no concept of what that means, but if f you go back to look at what I had with Kyle, that's the way I expressed what I felt for him is that I gave him sex.

I always wanted to. I had this thing about wanting to die, but yet, I was one of the strongest survivors that I know. My mother taught me to survive. That was the one thing that she taught me real well was how to survive. "You will survive in any given situation." I've survived the parish prisons in Louisiana, just being in there for like thirty days. They are holes. They are hell holes. They are hell holes. I mean they're nasty. We're talking about rats and cockroaches and bugs that you haven't ever seen, and like movie shit that they show how hard it is. I survived that and kept mentally focused.

Comment

You got to the end. Congratulations. The more we take it in, the more likely we are to stand up to the social forces that shape people who do with this man does. Did this story give you ideas about what to do? Then do it.

This is a classic case of an abused child becoming an abuser. This man became an abuser because no one helped him as a child. He has experienced complex trauma and NO ONE HELPED HIM. If anyone had been kind to him and had established a long-term relationship of trust with him and helped him deal with his many traumas, he would not have done what he did. He would not believe what he believes. Think about it, for goodness sake. Do something. Learn about attachment as the foundation for children learning to cope with trauma.

References and Sources

George the duck gets beat to death by thugs. YouTube. https://www.youtube.com/watch?v=4P17pELoRaE

Gilgun, Jane F. (2014, January 16). The Ducks of River Walk, San Antonio. YouTube. https://www.youtube.com/watch?v=T8o7LPi46HI

Gilgun, Jane F. (2013). The logic of murderous rampages. Amazon. http://www.amazon.com/Murderous-Rampages-Essays-Violence-Prevention/dp/1482039095/ref=la_B00458CS2G_1_17?s=books&ie=UTF8&qid=1389895641&sr=1-17

Gilgun, Jane F. (2012) *The NEATS: A child & family assessment* (2nd ed.). Amazon.

Gilgun, Jane F. (2011) *Child sexual abuse: From harsh realities to hope* (2nd ed). Amazon.

Kidd, Sue Monk. (2002). *The secret life of bees.* New York: Penguin.

Lieberman, Alicia F. (2004). Traumatic stress and quality of attachment: Reality and internalization in disorders of infant mental health. *Infant Mental Health Journal, 25(4),* 336-351.

National Child Traumatic Stress Network. http://www.nctsn.org/trauma-types/complex-trauma/assessment. Retrieved January 13, 2014.

Trauma Center a Division of Justice Resource Institute. http://www.traumacenter.org. Retrieved 11 January 2014.

Van der Kolk, Bessel A. (2005). Developmental Trauma Disorder: A new, rational diagnosis for children with complex trauma histories. *Psychiatric Annals 35(5),* 390-398. Available free on-line at http://www.traumacenter.org/products/pdf_files/preprint_dev_trauma_diso rder.pdf. Retrieved January 10, 2014.

11

"Be perfect, therefore, as your heavenly Father is perfect."

This is a homily I gave on February 27, 2014, at St. John's Episcopal Church, Linden Hills, Minnesota, USA.

I'm a deeply flawed human being, and God loves me. I'm also a deacon in formation at St. John's, about two-thirds of the way toward the diaconate.

God calls flawed human beings to do God's work. Moses had beaten an Egyptian to death and was in hiding when God called him to lead the Israelites out of Egypt. David committed adultery with Bathsheba and arranged to have Bathsheba's husband Uriah killed in battle. The apostles are famous for their thick-headedness.

How about Jesus? What he perfect? Matthew tells a story of the Canaanite woman who asked Jesus to cast a demon from her daughter. Jesus compared the woman to a dog. She stood up to him and argued back. Jesus recognized her great faith and repented. He cured her daughter at that moment.

How about Mary? As a child, the priests and nuns in my parish taught me she was perfect. The two jokes I remember are both about Mary's perfection. This is how one of them goes. Jesus was preaching to a crowd and said, "Let anyone who is without sin throw the first stone." A rock flew through the air and smacked Jesus right between the eyes. He yelled, "Mother."

God calls each of us to do God's work according to our gifts. Does Jesus really believe we can be perfect? Jesus knows we are predictably imperfect in relationship to God, others, and ourselves. He knows God is predictably faithful to us. At St. John's, we are reminded week in and week out that God loves us. We are made in the image and likeness of God. God saw that all creation is good, including us.

Many of us were raised in traditions that tell us we are sinners. We are descendants of Adam and Eve who ate the forbidden fruit. We are born in original sin and not in original goodness that the first chapter of Genesis tells us we are.

For many of us, sinfulness became our identity. Many, myself included, still felt guilty even though we were told that baptism and Jesus's agonizing death have saved us. Even going to confession didn't help. As a child, I felt guilty that Jesus died for my sins. Years later, in fits of frustration, I wondered, "Who asked him to?"

My career as a social worker has shown me how wide-spread the sense of being unworthy is. Abused and neglected children, battered women, adult survivors of trauma think they are bad. Think they must have done something to deserve being treated as they have been. It seems that being human means dealing with unworthiness.

Living into being made in God's image and likeness is a life-long journey. It's a process of becoming. It's a way of bringing the kingdom of God closer. It's seeing the divine in ourselves, others, and all of creation.

As some of you know, I am leading an oral history project at St. John's. A few months ago, I interviewed Bob Harvey, who is a former rector here and now rector emeritus. Bob said

> I didn't realize until not that many years ago that I hadn't really bought that God is present in me. I hadn't really bought that. And buying that has had a tremendous impact on me. Seeing that reality in other people changes how I deal with other people.

Henri Nouwen, a priest and theologian, has much to say about our status as God's beloved and the difficulties of living into God's love. Henri struggled with depression for most of his life. His own Roman Catholic church told him that he was unworthy because he was gay. He was concerned about self-rejection that happens when we internalize voices that call us worthless and unlovable.

Henri said

> Self-rejection is the greatest enemy of the spiritual life because it contradicts the sacred voice that calls us the 'Beloved.' Being the Beloved constitutes the core truth of our existence.

In today's Gospel, Jesus tells us to love our enemies and pray for those who persecute us. The negative voices we have internalized could be the enemies we most need to love and pray for.

I wonder how the world would change if every person began to love the enemy within. What does it take to have confidence in God's love for us? Can God's love help us to accept and make friends with our own sense of unworthiness and imperfections?

We can, with God's help. We can bring the kingdom of God closer.

But I wonder if we can do this perfectly. Can we be perfect as God is perfect?

What did Jesus mean?

The structure of Be perfect as your heavenly father is perfect is parallel in structure to the passage in Leviticus that we read for today: Be holy as I am holy. The audiences of Jesus's time would have immediately recalled the parallel structure and meaning. Today's Old Testament reading helps us to make similar connections.

Jesus used "tamim" for the word translated as "perfect." Tamim does not suggest moral perfection. As the word is used in other passages of Hebrew Scripture, it suggests wholeheartedness, reaching toward completion, a commitment to walking with God. For example, in a passage in Deuteronomy, the word "tamim "is translated as wholehearted, as in "You must be wholehearted with the Lord your God."

In our own time, being wholehearted is more doable than being perfect as God is perfect. Wholeheartedness is part of the commandment that Jesus said was the greatest: "Love the Lord your God with all your heart and with all your soul and with all your strength" and "love your neighbor as yourself."

Wholeheartedness is also the key word that Brené Brown uses in her internationally acclaimed research on coping with shame, vulnerability, imperfection, and unworthiness. Brené uses the word "wholehearted" to describe people who believe that they are loveable just as they are. Right now. Not next spring when we lost 10 pounds. Not when we finally get the perfect hair-do. Not when we get the next promotion and pay raise.

People who live wholeheartedly have a sense of belonging to something bigger than themselves. They have a spiritual life. They also have a sense of belonging to families, work, community, and religious institutions.

They are willing to feel their sense of unworthiness and vulnerability when these feelings arise, and they deal with them. They confide in persons who have earned their trust. They accept themselves as imperfect. They work on their self-rejection.

Experiencing our imperfections is humbling and often humiliating. A sense of humor about our shortcomings may help. Not only that, but it's hard to cope with the imperfections of others. It's easy to feel self-righteous, not turn the other cheek, even to seek revenge and to retaliate. It's much easier to wish others would change and not us. It can seem impossible to be gracious to those we experience as ungracious.

We can't transform ourselves all at once. In asking us to be perfect as God as perfect. Jesus urges us to have a sense of direction, to reach toward completion, to know that God loves us and walks with us. When we do this, we are wholehearted in our love of God in whose image and likeness we already are.

References

Brown, Brené (2010-09-20). *The Gifts of Imperfection: Let Go of Who You Think You're Supposed to Be and Embrace Who You Are* (Kindle Locations 76-77). Hazelden Publishing. Kindle Edition.

Ford, Michael (2009). *The Wounded Prophet: A Portrait of Henri J. M. Nouwen.* New York: Doubleday.

Tamim: Wholehearted with God. Hebrew for Christians website. http://search.atomz.com/search/?sp-a=sp10030011&sp-f=iso-8859-1&sp-p=all&sp-q=tamim&FormsButton3=Search. D

12

We are the Baby in the Manger

This is a sermon I gave at Trinity Episcopal Church, Excelsior, Minnesota, USA, on 12 December 2014. I paraphrased Walter Bruggemann's poem because I don't have permission to cite the poem.

In the name of the one who loves us

"The light shines in the darkness, and the darkness did not overcome it."

Our Judeo-Christian heritage reminds us time and again that there is one God. We are made in the image and likeness of God. God loves us. We are to love God with our whole hearts, souls, minds, and strength. We are to love ourselves, others, and our enemies. God is the life that resides in all things and connects all things. God is good. God is spirit. God is light. God is love. God is everywhere. And there's more. We seek God. We long for God. God longs for us. God wants to save us. God is the source. God is the beginning. God is the end.

Our loving God is relentless. God is determined to claim us as the beloved. So God gave us Jesus as yet another lesson on how to love God, ourselves, others, and enemies. This Christmas season reminds us of how tricky God is. God seduces us with a newborn child, wrapped in swaddling clothes and lying in a manger. Don't you imagine the infant Jesus bathed in light, smiling, gurgling, his arms and legs moving, looking into your eyes? Do you feel something in your heart?

God did not stop wooing us with a beautiful baby. No, the drama and poignancy of the story draw us in further. Mary is young, pregnant and unmarried. Joseph is subject to public shame because, from appearances, Mary is pregnant by another man. He considers putting her away as was his right. He chooses to remain with Mary and be a father to the unborn child.

Mary and Joseph travel through a harsh mountainous desert in the cold dark of winter only to find there is no place for them to stay. "A hard time they had of it," "Just the worst time of year" (Eliot). Jesus is born in a barn, surrounded by soft-eyed cattle. Was there water to bathe the newborn? Did Mary sit in a warm bath after the birth?

The story goes on. The shepherds, the star, the Magi, exile in Egypt to save Jesus from death at the hands of Herod.

Writing teachers could use this story to show students how to build suspense and drama. Conflict, hard times, joy. It's all there.

Today's readings set a context for the story of the birth of Jesus. They remind us of the complexities of what it means to love God and what it means for God to love us. Incarnation, light, love, trust in God, and salvation on the one hand. On the other are hard times, danger, and rejection.

As John wrote in today's Gospel, "the world did not know him." Jesus was the son of God, and the Roman authorities crucified him. They mistook the good for the bad.

What about us? What about our misperceptions? Do we mistake the good for the bad? Examples abound. An instance for today is the perception of some white police officers. They see unarmed black men as dangerous. The man who murdered two police officers saw them not as men doing their jobs, but as enemies who deserved to die. The Pakistani Taliban murdered 142 school children and six adults a few weeks ago. What did they think they were doing? They must have thought they were doing something good.

Sometimes we hurt others and ourselves out of good intentions. Many people seek the American dream, follow scripts of accomplishment and accolades. Some of us chase the next best thing. We neglect our families and our children for the sake of scripts that tell us what is important. Through God's grace, we may realize our accomplishments are not enough. Things are not enough. External praise is not enough. We misperceive what is good for us and for those we love.

As Sally Brown said in last Sunday's sermon, we become sick and tired and then sick and tired of being sick and tired. We realize how powerless we are. We change our lives, with God's help. A sign of our transformation is the trust we put in God. We place the one God in the center of our lives, not accomplishments and not external praise.

Sometimes we don't misperceive. We do have hard times, just as Mary and Joseph did in the Christmas story. People we love suffer, become ill, are injured, die. We become frail in our old age. We lose our jobs. We are estranged from people we love. Millions of children are abused and neglected every day. The list goes on. Sexual assault in marriage, in families, in dating, on the streets, and in war. Terrorism. Mass murder. Refugees flee their homes to save their lives. The exploitation of undocumented workers. Deportation. Separation from children. Yes, we have hard times. They are not misperceptions.

The issue is what we do with our hard times. How do we find the light? How do we find God's healing love? In a poem called "People of Many Secrets," Walter Brueggeman reflects upon the kinds of suffering that everyone experiences, each in our own ways.

In order for us to understand the pain and suffering of others, we must know our own pain and suffering and not keep them a secret from ourselves, which we often do without realizing it. Prayer, meditation, and spiritual direction help us to uncover our secrets. As spiritual leaders point out, doing so is difficult and painful; we relive the suffering that earlier in our lives was so painful that we repressed it. It takes great faith to uncover our secrets.

According to Christian theology, none of our secrets are hidden from God. Brueggerman said our secrets are our truths. We must tell them for the sake of our own lives and for the lives of others. Brueggerman provides a list of our secrets that are our truths: "grief unresolved," "pain unacknowledged," "fear," "hate," "being taken advantage of," "being used, and manipulated, and slandered."

Prayer, meditation, spiritual direction, and gathering together for the Eucharist help us to uncover our secrets. As spiritual leaders point out, doing so is difficult. We relive the suffering that earlier in our lives was so painful that we repressed it. It takes great faith to uncover our secrets. God waits patiently for us.

We experience healing when we know our own truths, own them, and allow God's love to touch our hurts and our hearts.

With God's help, we let go of our hurts and the dreams and the things that do not satisfy. As we do, we make room in our hearts for God. We experience in our hearts that we are made in the image and likeness of

God, and so is everyone else. We become more centered and more peaceful. "Come to me... and I will give you rest" (Matthew 11:28). We also deepen our capacities for empathy. We no longer keep silent (Isaiah 62: 1). For the love of God, we seek the well-being of others. We are not perfect at it, but we get better at it as we pray, meditate, and grow spiritually.

Brueggeman calls Jesus "the best kept secret of hurt." I don't know what Brueggeman means, but when I first read it, I felt it in my heart. "Jesus is the best kept secret of hurt." Each of us may have our own interpretations. I will share mine with you.

Jesus's love of God led him to love others and to see their hurt. His love moved him to respond to hurt. Not only did he respond to the hurt he experienced in individuals, but also to the oppressive practices that caused the hurt. The cross and crucifixion are both symbolic and concrete representations of the hurt that Jesus took on and the hurt of all of us, all of humankind. Jesus experienced incarnation and resurrection. He opened to us the possibilities that we too can experience incarnation and resurrection. God pours his love into our hearts (Romans 5: 5).

If we as individuals, experience the cross, resurrection, and incarnation deep within, we are in touch with the processes that lead us to God. If we dig deep, we can tap into our own goodness and love. When we speak from our hearts, we may touch the hearts of others. Others in turn may uncover their own hurts and their own truths. They too may make more room for God in their hearts.

As John wrote in today's Gospel, "to all who received him, who believed in his name, he gave power to become children of God, who were born, not of blood or of the will of the flesh or of the will of man, but of God" (John 1:12).

This season of Christmas reminds us of these truths. Each of us is the baby in the manger. We are naked, helpless, and totally dependent on the loving God. Imagine how the world would change if each of us experienced this Jesus in ourselves and in others.

Blessed be God forever.

References

Brueggemann, Walter (2001). *Awed to Heaven, Rooted in Earth: Prayers of Walter Brueggemann* (Kindle Locations 238-244). Kindle Edition.

Brueggemann, Walter (2001) *The Prophetic Imagination* (2nd ed.). Minneapolis: Fortress.

Eliot, T.S. (1962). The journey of the magi. In *T. S. Eliot, The complete poems and plays*. New York: Harcourt Brace.

Gilgun, Jane F. (2014). Responses to Hackenberg: Was Jesus a prophet for young Jewish men only? Wordpress. Professorjane.wordpress.com

13

Killing Feels Good:
Reflections on a Daddy Long Legs Spider

I just killed a daddy long legs spider, whacked it with the back of a brush It felt good to crush that arachnid. When I spotted it, brush was already in hand.

I smacked it, thinking you are probably related to the spider that bit me a four weeks ago. How that bite hurt and kept hurting. It felt good to strike you. You broke crooked bits. Your legs looked like legs.

I came back to myself. There it is, plain in front of me; I just took pleasure in killing not the one who hurt me but a similar creature.

Scapegoating? Revenge? Just desserts? Instinct? Part of being human? I don't know I just know it felt good at the time.

Would I do it again?

Violence as Good
For Those Who Commit It:
A Reader
2nd edition
by Jane Gilgun

ISBN-13: 978-1506175560
ISBN-10:1506175562

Many of these essays were first published on Amazon and scribd.com .

Key words: violence, violence prevention, violence as good, shame,
etiology of violence, violence prevention, child sexual abuse, sex offenders,
resilience, qualitative research

About the Author

Jane F. Gilgun, PhD, LICSW, is a professor, School of Social Work, University of Minnesota, Twin Cities, USA. She does research on the meanings of violence to perpetrators, the development of violent behaviors, and how persons overcome adversities. She has published widely in these areas and on qualitative methods within the Chicago School of Sociology tradition.

She worked at a public Rhode Island child welfare social service agency for several years, returned to graduate school, and then became a professor. She also writes children's books, non-fiction, and articles that are available on Amazon and other internet booksellers. She has many videos on YouTube that include the landscapes in Northwest Ireland, trail riding in Minnesota and elsewhere, horse racing, pig racing, and more.

Her interests include her horses, Padron's Elegante (Ellie) and Finn MacCool, who are mother and son, her dog Jazz, gardening, photography, cooking, the arts, and spending time in County Leitrim and County Sligo, Ireland.

Jane has a bachelor's and master's in English and American poetry from the Catholic University of America and the University of Rhode Island, respectively, a master's in social work from the University of Chicago, a licentiate in family studies and sexuality from the Catholic University of Louvain, Belgium, and a Ph.D. in child and family studies from Syracuse University. She is a licensed independent clinical social worker.

www.ingramcontent.com/pod-product-compliance
Lightning Source LLC
Chambersburg PA
CBHW071221280526
45787CB00002B/755